Called to Caregiving

A Resource for Equipping Deacons in the Believers Church

Edited by June A. Gibble and Fred W. Swartz

BRETHREN PRESS
Elgin, Illinois

Called to Caregiving
A Resource for Equipping Deacons in the Believers Church

Cover design: Jim Massman

Project participants: Brethren in Christ Church, Church of the Brethren, General Conference Mennonite Church, Mennonite Church, Mennonite Brethren Church.

Library of Congress Cataloging-in-Publication Data

Called to caregiving.

  Bibliography: p.
  1. Deacons—Church of the Brethren. 2. Deacons—Mennonites. 3. Deacons—Brethren in Christ Church. 4. Caring—Religious aspects—Christianity. 5. Church of the Brethren—Government. 6. Mennonites—Government. 7. Brethren in Christ Church—Government. I. Gibble, June A. (June Adams) II. Swartz, Fred W., 1938-
BX7826.C35 1987 262'.14973 87-25601
ISBN 0-87178-150-6

Manufactured in the United States of America

Contents

SECTION FIVE:
SAMPLES OF CONGREGATIONAL DEACON MINISTRIES

SECTION SIX:
APPENDIX

SECTION SEVEN:
ANNOTATED BIBLIOGRAPHY AND RESOURCES

Writers

Harold E. Bauman
Elkhart, Indiana - Associate Secretary for Congregational Leadership and Worship for the Mennonite Board of Congregational Ministries of the Mennonite Church.

Anita Smith Buckwalter
Lansing, Michigan - Co-Pastor of Lansing Church of the Brethren, Chairwoman of the Church of the Brethren General Board.

Joan George Deeter
North Manchester, Indiana - Executive, Parish Ministries Commission of the Church of the Brethren General Board, former pastor of West Manchester Church.

Al Dueck
Fresno, California - Author, and Professor of Pastoral Care, Mennonite Brethren Biblical Seminary.

June Adams Gibble
Elgin, Illinois - Chaplain, free lance editor, and former editor for Parish Ministries Commission, Church of the Brethren General Board.

Jonathan C. Hunter
San Diego, California - Free lance writer, former pastor at Harrisburg, Pennsylvania.

Neta Jackson
Evanston, Illinois - Author, writer, and member of the Brethren-Mennonite affiliated Reba Place Fellowship.

Clarence Isaac Kulp, Jr.
Vernfield, Pennsylvania - Author, historian, and lecturer on Brethren-Mennonite history and folklore.

James M. Lapp
Lombard, Illinois - Executive Secretary of the Mennonite Church General Board, former Campus Minister at Goshen College.

John E. Lapp
Souderton, Pennsylvania - Former Bishop of Franconia Conference, acknowledged Mennonite historian.

Larry Martens
Fresno, California - President of Mennonite Brethren Biblical Seminary and Associate Professor of Pastoral Care.

Donald E. Miller
Elgin, Illinois - General Secretary of the Church of the Brethren General Board, former Brightbill Professor of Ministry at Bethany Theological Seminary.

Karen Peterson Miller
Carol Stream, Illinois - Writer, volunteer staff for People of the Covenant, and doctoral student in education.

Lenora H. Stern
Mechanicsburg, Pennsylvania - Adult educator, Coordinator for Child and Adolescent Services System's Program in Pennsylvania.

Fred W. Swartz
Manassas, Virginia - Pastor of Manassas Church of the Brethren, former editor for the General Services Commission, Church of the Brethren General Board.

Erland Waltner
Elkhart, Indiana - Executive Secretary for Mennonite Medical Association, former President of Associated Mennonite Biblical Seminaries.

(Writers for Section Five "Samples of Congregational Deacon Ministries," are identified with their respective articles.)

Preface

The presence of deacons was a mixed blessing during my eighteen years of pastoral ministry. In my early years as pastor, relating to and with deacons was sometimes precarious; at times we were supportive friends but, at other times, the deacons as a body seemed like a "strong immovable force" blocking my "creative pastoral enterprises!"

Not only was the relationship between deacons and myself unpredictable; the relationship between the deacon body and the congregation was also uncertain. At times the deacons were accused by congregational persons as "gossiping meddlers" and at other times the organizational structures almost seemed to declare deacons as non-essential.

Such "deacon displacement" was dramatically illustrated when a deacon chairperson concluded his report to the congregational business meeting with the shocking recommendation to "disband the deacon body." This actually happened at a congregational meeting soon after I became pastor of the Ambler Church of the Brethren. Actually, the recommendation to disband was a "cry for identity and place," and fortunately no action was taken. Prior to that meeting the deacons had been asked to study the Undershepherd Plan, but the message some deacons heard was: "You're not doing your job as deacons—we need undershepherds to replace you." So the recommendation to disband!

As the new pastor, not yet caught up in a congregation/deacon/pastor power struggle, I was able to recommend a compromise of substituting the name "deacon" for "undershepherd" and calling ours a "geographic deacon plan." I can still hear the positive responses. Immediately the entire deacon body warmed up to the concept as they sensed a renewed place and purpose for deacons in the life of the congregation. That marked the beginning of a mutually supportive deacon-pastoral team relationship, one which has continued even beyond my being their pastor.

Thus, out of my personal and pastoral history has come my strong belief that the team ministry of deacons and pastor can and should be a positive force in the nurturing of persons to wholeness of life in Jesus Christ. And, likewise, this is the belief that undergirds the development of this resource, *Called to Caregiving: A Resource for Equipping Deacons in the Believers Church.*

The assignment for developing this resource grew out of a denominational objective to develop materials for the training of deacons consistent with the 1983 Church of the Brethren Annual Conference paper, "The

Office of Deacon." As the staff person responsible for implementing that objective, I invited the Brethren/Mennonite Mental Health Awareness and Education Committee to sponsor the project as an Anabaptist cooperative endeavor. Accepting that proposal, the group then appointed a sub-committe of Conrad Wetzel, Joan Deeter, and myself to develop a training resource. Shortly thereafter, June Adams Gibble was recruited as project consultant and editor.

Included in the process for developing this resource was a Deacon Consultation at the Elkhart Church of the Brethren. Invited representatives from the Brethren in Christ Church, the General Conference Mennonite Church, the Mennonite Brethren Church, and the Mennonite Church joined the Church of the Brethren at this consultation, where a decision was made that these five denominations would jointly sponsor this deacon resourcing project.

Following the Elkhart consultation, key persons were appointed from each of the sponsoring denominations to oversee the development of this resource. Included were Owen H. Alderfer, Harold Bauman, Al Dueck, Erland Waltner, plus the continuing planning committee of Joan Deeter, June Gibble, Conrad Wetzel, and myself. It was agreed that my office would assume major responsibilities in the contracting with writers and overall supervision. Somewhat later, Fred Swartz was recruited as a second editor, with Fred assuming responsibility as manuscript and reading editor, and June Gibble as the layout and publishing editor. The two of them have worked closely together, and with my office, in the development of the resource.

Important too was the receiving of a financial grant from the Mennonite Mutual Aid Association. Receiving that grant made possible the publishing of an attractive resource at an affordable price. We are indeed grateful to Mennonite Mutual Aid for their generous support.

Many persons have influenced the shaping of *Called to Caregiving: A Resource for Equipping Deacons in the Believers Church.* I am personally appreciative to my Parish Ministries colleagues, the Parish Ministries Commission, and Ralph McFadden, Parish Ministries Executive, for continuous support and assistance. My secretary, Virginia Eldredge, has given invaluable hours in manuscript preparation. Also important were the nearly forty readers from all five denominations who critiqued the manuscripts at various times. And most important were the writers to whom we are indebted for providing the content.

Finally, I wish to acknowledge the countless numbers of deacons and pastors who requested such a resource and encouraged our work. While it is certain that this is not the final word, it is hoped that this may be an important resource in the equipping of deacons for their caregiving ministry in the latter days of the 20th century.

Jay A. Gibble
Project Coordinator
Parish Ministries Staff for Health and Welfare
Church of the Brethren General Board

Introduction

You have been called to be a deacon. Now what do you do? Maybe more importantly, what are you to *be*? Perhaps you remember the deacons of a generation or two ago. For the most part they were stalwart men who were the primary movers and shakers in the congregation. Or perhaps you are too young to remember deacons *ever* taking a significant role in your congregation; maybe there were no deacons at all!

Whichever concept of deacons you hold, let us challenge you to erase that picture and begin a new profile on your mind's slate. First of all, we shall operate from the understanding that the word "deacon" applies to both male and female holders of the office. The New Testament uses the same word, *diakonos*, both for men and women who are deacons, implying that both share in the same duties and each is entitled to all the respects of the office in his or her own right.

Secondly, the denomination of which you are a member has committed itself to a reclamation of the office of deacon in the congregation. To be sure, there is a rich precedent and heritage for deacons both in the New Testament and in the historical development of Anabaptist faith. But in the past several decades, deacons generally have not been regarded as major leaders in congregational life and ministry. That has had its unfortunate consequences, such as contributing toward membership decline, reducing the amount of vital care a congregation can give its members, and providing fewer models of disciplined spiritual life within the church.

The new emphasis on deacons for the Brethren in Christ, the Church of the Brethren, and the Mennonite family of churches picks up as a central focus for the office the function of *caregiving*. Caregiving is not all that deacons do, but it is the overarching commission of the deacon's call. Deacons are to function as "ministers" in the congregation—extensions of the *paraclete*, the Comforter, (John 14:16,26), embodying Christ's love for others amidst the tensions and trials of the age.

We hope that this resource, *Called to Caregiving: A Resource for Equipping Deacons in the Believers Church*, will help you "catch" the spirit and importance of the deacon's role as caregiver, as well as provide a practical design for training you to be a caregiver.

The first section, "The Congregation As a Caring Community," seeks to place the deacon's task within the whole mission and family of the congregation. No leader in the church operates in a vacuum; each is a servant in the one purpose of the church—to help all people experience, receive, and respond to the love and truth of Jesus Christ. Lenora Stern in her article, "A Call to Caring," says this requires intentionality as caregivers: taking the initiative to love—even those who otherwise do not appeal to us, getting involved in meeting the needs of others, and a strong commitment to be a follower of Jesus Christ.

Larry Martens, in "The Caring Congregation," identifies several sources of caregiving in the congregation, with one critical source being the deacon. His seven marks of a caring congregation are important points to ponder.

Al Dueck's article, "The Caregiving Team," helps us define the thoroughness of caregiving that the congregation can offer when the gifts and training of many different caregivers are recognized and utilized. It is essential for the deacon to be part of a team within the congregation, a team of persons who are combining roles to fulfill Christ's commission.

Section Two, "The Role of Deacons in History," surveys the heritage of the Anabaptist tradition and the connection between our modern practice and that of the deacons in the earliest church.

Erland Waltner, author of "A Brief Biblical/Historical Perspective," examines first the New Testament origin of the office of deacon and the deacon's role as "one who serves." Then he traces the application of the biblical model in both formal and informal branches of the developing church. The bottom line, he discovers, is that the call of the deacon has always been held to be a high and holy one.

Harold E. Bauman, in "Variations in Anabaptist Traditions" explores the place of deacons in the leadership structures of Anabaptist communions. He discovers that the role of deacons has varied considerably over the years, and that the new interest is in having deacons who do deacon ministry so that the pastor and the elders can give spiritual oversight to congregational life and mission.

Section Two closes with an insightful interview with two keen observers of the historical function of deacons. In "Remembering How It Was," June A. Gibble finds out from Clarence Kulp of the Church of the Brethren and John Lapp of the Mennonite Church that deacons were premier officers of the 18th and 19th century Anabaptist congregations. They were heavily involved with "administering" and "disciplining," and they may have assumed too much authority. But both analysts agree that no other office in the church can effect unity and caring within the congregation to the degree the deacon can.

Section Three "Reclaiming the Office of Deacon" is intended to make a strong case for the validity and revitalization of the deacon office in today's church. Fred W. Swartz' article, "The Image and Ministry of Deacons Within the Congregation," calls for reinstating deacons as "ministers," as opposed to "managers." Deacons should be called with the help of the Holy Spirit to a significant task for the congregation.

Jonathan C. Hunter, who contributes the article entitled "Deacons: An Integral Part of Pastoral Ministry," discusses the close relationship pastors and deacons must maintain to effectively give pastoral care to the congregation. In fact, pastors and deacons are both models and ministers to each other in effective caregiving.

Karen Peterson Miller, in "The Annual Deacon Visit: A Form of Pastoral Care," examines the values of the historical deacon practice of making an annual visit to each member of the congregation and proposes a new version of the same for today.

Donald E. Miller offers a truly contemporary concept, hospitality, as a vital element of the deacon's caregiving. In "Deacon Hospitality: A Holy Calling," he finds the basis for this idea from the biblical accounts of welcoming the stranger and caring for those with special needs.

Joan George Deeter believes that the vicarious suffering of Christ is repeated in the lives of his followers, as they too experience the "valleys" and "deserts" of human existence. "Deacons: Channels of God's Healing Spirit" lifts up a most meaningful and tender ministry for deacons.

Then follows the summary article of Section Three, "The Caregiving Functions of Deacons" written by Anita Smith Buckwalter. This article examines seven deacon functions: serving, nurturing, healing, worshipping, discipling, presence, and advocating. Practical definitions for each function are given.

Section Four, "The Training of Deacons," provides both a rationale and a design for training deacons for their caregiving task. In "Elements of a Deacon Training Program," James M. Lapp lists six important elements for a comprehensive deacon training program, including personal growth, modeling, teaching, apprenticeship, evaluation, and support and renewal.

Then comes a "how to" section, "Training Sessions for Equipping Deacons." Neta Jackson has written a curriculum for six training sessions that can be used in a variety of settings. The activities and study get the deacon personally involved in "catching" the role of caregiver and being equipped to carry it out. The author skillfully uses the materials in Sections One to Three of this resource. These training sessions should be used by every deacon group as soon as possible.

Finally, the reader will find additional practical material in Section Five, "Samples of Congregational Deacon Ministries," and in Sections Six, "Appendix," and Seven, "Annotated Bibliography." *Materials marked "sample" in the Appendix (pp. 163-170) are intended for reproduction and may be copied or reproduced without permission from the publisher.*

It is obvious, as one reads how congregations and even denominations structure their deacon programs, that the design and nature of deacon ministry must be adapted to meet the needs of each local community. It is the purpose of this resource to offer a variety of models for an effective caregiving ministry. We hope it will help you find your mission for your calling.

Fred W. Swartz
Pastor, Manassas, VA
Church of the Brethren

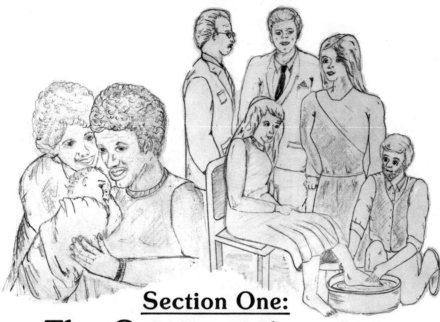

Section One:
The Congregation as a Caring Community

A Call to Caring

Lenora Stern

A new commandment I give you: Love one another. As I have loved you, so you must love one another. All men will know that you are my disciples if you love one another (John 13:34-35 NIV).

Jesus shared this significant teaching with his disciples just before his arrest. Throughout his ministry, Jesus had been teaching his disciples that love was the key in relationships—it was an attitude and action which demonstrated caring for one another.

We who are Jesus' disciples today, who are in fact the church, have much to offer to a broken and groping world. Specifically, we offer the love and caring, the optimism and hope, and the courage and joy which result from our personal relationship with Christ. We have opportunities to be caring persons in many contexts, including the family, the church, the community. We have a special call to be caregivers within the local church family, the congregation. Our focus in this article is to discover how we can live out Jesus' new commandment that we love one another.

I suggest that we, as disciples, need to be *assertive servants* in caring for others in the family, in the congregation, and in the neighborhood. To understand the term *assertive servant*, we note that Webster defines a servant as "one who exerts himself to the benefit of another." The term assertive implies that one makes an intentional choice to act, to get involved, to help others. So an assertive servant is a person who intentionally chooses to act in a way that benefits another. An assertive servant acts out of an attitude of caring.

We often ask children, "What do you want to be when you grow up?" We also need to ask ourselves, "What am I becoming, now that I am an adult?" Am I a giver or a taker—a mover and a shaker or one who needs to be shaken—an affirmer/encourager or an evaluator/criticizer? Who am I in my relating with others?

In his book, *The Second Greatest Commandment,* William Fletch summarizes the important characteristics of Christ's love which were demonstrated in his life and ministry:

Jesus was concerned about individuals, families, homes, and health;

Jesus was willing to take time for needy people even though he was so busy and often surrounded by crowds;

Jesus provided faithful support by praying for individuals who were struggling in their spiritual lives;

Jesus offered complete forgiveness, even when it seemed undeserved;

Jesus humbly served his followers, as demonstrated in his washing the disciples' feet;

Jesus ultimately gave himself in death for his people.

From this list we can see that Jesus modeled a very practical brand of love, one that ministered to the pressing needs of his followers. Thus, Jesus is a perfect example of the assertive servant. Our challenge as Jesus' disciples today is to learn how to focus our primary concern on the needs of others after the life-giving ideal he demonstrated.

Being an assertive servant who practices Christ-like caring is not easy. It demands that we give ourselves totally to God, and then extend ourselves fully to our brothers and sisters. We are given the command: "Whoever loves God must also love his brother" (1 John 4:21 NIV). Most of the time it is easy to love a child; as children grow older, it often becomes more difficult to find ways to express our love for them. And with adults it may be even more difficult to know how to show caring love. But, in spite of the difficulty, we must not lose our creativity for and our commitment to finding ways to care for people.

Christians are to love every brother and sister whether or not the love is returned. In fact, as Christians we are to extend love even to those whose lifestyle or behavior is undesirable, rather than confine our love only to those who mirror our own values (Matt. 5:46-47). Note 1 Peter 3:8: "Finally, all of you, live in harmony with one another; be sympathetic, love as brothers, be compassionate and humble. Do not repay evil with evil or insult with insult, but with blessing. . ." (NIV). How well do we, as Jesus' disciples, model and assist others in learning to return good (a blessing) in a negative situation? For certain, the call to being an assertive servant is risky!

A story of several assertive servants is found in Mark 2:1-12. Four men carried their friend to Jesus to be healed. Michael Slater, in his book, *The Stretcher Bearers*, notes that the paralytic man truly needed his wonderfully determined friends to carry him and his problem to the feet of Jesus.

If we understand this concept of the assertive servant, then the miracle which took place in Mark 2 can take place in our lives. Because the healing in this story occurred, not primarily because of the man on the stretcher, nor because Jesus had the gifts to heal; the healing took place because of the faith, encouragement, and support of the man's compassionate friends (assertive servants). They cared; they were determined to find an answer to each problem as it arose: finding the home where Jesus was, knowing where and how to cut the hole in the roof, and how to lower their friend down to where Jesus was. Jesus saw their determination and their faith, and he healed their friend.

Opportunities to be caring and assertive servants are still with us today, as the following poem shows. The question is: How do we respond?

> I was hungry and you formed a humanities club
>   to discuss my hunger.
>   *thank you.*
> I was imprisoned and you crept off quietly
>   to your chapel to pray for my release.
>   *nice.*
> I was naked and in your mind you debated the
>   morality of my appearance.
>   *what good did that do?*
> I was sick and you knelt and thanked God for
>   your health.
>   *but I needed you.*
> I was homeless and you preached to me of the
>   shelter of the love of God.
>   *I wish you had taken me home.*
> I was lonely and you left me alone to pray for me.
>   *why didn't you stay?*
> You seem so holy, so close to God; but I'm still
>   very hungry, lonely, cold, and still in pain.
>   *does it matter?*
>
> —Anonymous

We are called to live out "New Testament" caring—involvement, assertiveness, persistency, faith, hope, and optimism. The result of such caring is great joy in the life of the individual, the family, the congregation, and the neighborhood.

Let us recommit ourselves as Jesus' followers to becoming assertive servants. Let us seek the Lord and accept his love in our own lives. Let us pray for sensitivity and creativity in knowing how to care for people. Let us take relationship risks. Most of all, let us share the fullness of God's love with others. Then, we shall be obedient and assertive servants!

The Caring Congregation

Larry Martens

My wife, Kathleen, and I experienced the love and support of a caring congregation first hand. We were expecting our first child. The pregnancy went well; the anticipation was high. Kathleen gave birth to an eight pound boy. Our excitement, however, was short-lived. For three days the infant struggled for life, then died. An autopsy revealed a congenital heart condition. We need not describe to you the devastation and pain we felt.

The extent of the Christian community's response to our need was beyond our expectation. There was an outpouring of love from family, friends, and members of the congregation where we served. People—some we barely knew—sent flowers, cards, and letters. Other couples who had lost a child through death talked about their loss with us and encouraged us. Many stopped by to say, "We care." While the pastor also cared for us, it was the corporate expression of the priestly ministry of many people in the congregation which impressed us. Indeed, the *church* cared for us.

Such caring within the congregation is essential. The unmet human needs in every church and community are so numerous and varied that a pastor alone can meet only a small fraction of the needs. A congregation fully involved in caring for the lonely, sick, aging, bereaved, homebound, institutionalized, exploited, and socially and economically oppressed people in the community multiplies the ministry of the congregation. When members of the congregation reach out as "informal" priests they become the church, the body of Christ, serving those in need.

Caregiving in the congregation comes from three sources: (1) professionally-trained pastoral counselors, psychotherapists, and other specialists; (2) the pastor and selected laypersons such as deacons or elders; and (3) the congregation. While many people do see the church as an important vehicle for care, most people view source one, professionally-trained specialists, as providing the most effective care. Many of these professionals regard source two as a valid source of care, but yet they often suspect the motivation of church and clergy. Current pastoral care literature and practice in the church emphasize source two as the *primary* source of pastoral care. Unfortunately, source three, the congregation, is rarely recognized as an adequate and effective response to the need for care.

While I do not minimize the importance of the first two sources, I believe that a reordering of the sources of caregiving is needed to adequately reflect a biblical model of ministry. The congregation must become the primary source for caregiving.

The concept of the congregation as primary caregiver takes seriously our biblical and theological tradition. From that tradition we can identify seven marks of a caring congregation.

1. The congregation as caregiver views ministry as the work of God through God's people.

The church does not constitute its own ministry; the ministry is given (2 Cor. 5:18-19). The caring ministry, therefore, is not rooted in routine human events; it is rooted in the ongoing work of Christ among his people. Kingdom citizens serve in the awareness that Christ is at work through his people healing the hurting, the broken, the suffering, and the guilty.

Whenever and wherever there are possibilities for the community of faith to share in meeting human need, caring congregations see this as the work of God. It is not something they do on their own; it is something Christ does in them, through them, with them (2 Cor. 4:1-7). The people of God respond to the hurts and pains of others not because it is the humanitarian thing to do, but because they are servants of Christ who willingly hazard risk and become vulnerable for the sake of those in need.

2. The congregation as caregiver believes that all Christians have a ministry because they are Christians.

Ministry is a word which comes from the Greek term *diakonos,* meaning "one who serves." It refers not to a special office but to a special function. It is a ministry given not to a special class of people but exercised by *every* man and woman who follows Christ (1 Cor. 12; 1 Pet. 2:9-10).

The church often finds itself confused over the issue. Don't we hire pastors to shepherd the church and minister to its need? Indeed! Pastors do care for people in crisis. But ministry is not the function of a few multi-gifted persons who serve. Rather, ministry is the work of a multi-gifted body intended by God for a priestly ministry. All Christians are servants called to minister to people in need. Carlyle Marney is right when he says that no professional clergy can do all that the church is called to do. Care is not the function of an exclusive class of ordained persons who are the designated caregivers of the church. The life-signs of the Spirit in the body of Christ are not the prerogative of clergy; they are the privilege and responsibility of all followers of Christ.

3. The congregation as caregiver assumes a corporate rather than an individual context.

Much of pastoral care literature depicts the caring relationship as taking place in a one-on-one context. Terms such as "shepherd," "priest," and "pastor" reflect images of individual care. On the other hand, terms such as "the people of God," "the body of Christ," "the *koinonia,*" and "the household of faith" are corporate images for describing caring relationships in the human context.

The corporate images emphasize the group rather than isolated individuals. They reflect family bondedness and solidarity among members of the group. Human autonomy or individualism is absent in the interpersonal dynamics of the community of faith. Rather, there is an interdependence, expressed in various ways. Kinship and family ties take on new meaning as people view each other as brothers and sisters (Matt. 18:15). Members are sensitive to one another and act caringly when others suffer or rejoice (1 Cor. 12:25-26). All members of the body stimulate one another for service (Eph. 4:11-23), encourage each other toward spiritual maturity (Eph. 4:16), share one another's pain and hurt in spiritual failure (Gal. 6:2), and function as priests for one another (1 Pet. 2:9).

4. The congregation as caregiver is expressed through the sharing of diverse gifts.

The Body of Christ suggests that a variety of persons, each uniquely gifted by God's Spirit, graces the community of faith with special ministries. Each ministry is needed for community wholeness and maturity. Since each believer is gifted by the Holy Spirit, each person is called to ministry. Every person *has* a ministry and *is* a minister. Every member has unique caring opportunities. Each member has gifts which uniquely reflect the spiritual graces given each person by the Holy Spirit for ministry (1 Cor. 12:7-11).

Such expressions of spiritual giftedness reflect the interpersonal character of ministry. The one who receives care and the caregiver often both give and receive care within the same caring experience. Care within the body of Christ is, therefore, a double call to discipleship in which persons are called into a community of love and service and at the same time are asked to cultivate the capacity to be ministered to by others. Those who care, receive; those who receive, care. Accordingly, those who receive have the *need* to give; those who give have the *need* to receive. This reciprocal process is based on community solidarity, wherein each person is free to both give and receive in an atmosphere of openness and trust. This relationship requires a selflessness that permits the needs of others to become a priority.

5. The congregation as caregiver reflects a shared life.

The term *koinonia* (fellowship) in the New Testament means to share in something with someone. Paul used the term to describe a spiritual unity in which the Christian community is bound together not by some common ethnic origin or by social status, but by the reality of a common faith in Christ (Gal. 3:28). This spiritual unity or fellowship is expressed interpersonally in concrete and often sacrificial ways where hurts, struggles, burdens, and concerns are shared in an atmosphere of mutual support and trust. The care expressed, however, is more than mere sentiment or kindly feeling; it often is manifested in the form of a gift or deed.

6. The congregation as caregiver takes seriously family relationships and commitments.

The church as a caring community reflects in its life and experience the concept of the church as family. The metaphor of the household of faith is taken seriously. Members of the community are a cohesive family unit. They view each other as sons and daughters of the King and brothers and sisters of the community of the King (Mark 3:33-35, John 1:12, Rom. 8:14-15).

The image of the household expresses the concept of the extended family rather than the nuclear family. Church family life provides a sense of belonging for people who experience alienation and estrangement. It is a cohesive community free of all barriers of race, status, or condition. Family members express endearment and friendship for one another, and nurture each other with encouragement and care. Care within the congregational family is expressed more informally than formally; it is more spontaneous than planned; it is more improvised than ordered; it is more impromptu than orchestrated. Family care focuses on family needs and is characterized by family dynamics practiced in an atmosphere of love and acceptance.

7. Care is the measure of a congregation's effectiveness.

Our Lord gave us the way of love and compassion. Nothing is more central to the church's calling. Love and compassion are to dominate our character as a church community. Indeed, God is a God of compassion who identifies fully with us in our confusion, pain, and sinfulness, and responds to our need with grace and love. And, God calls us to be people of compassion who respond to one another even as God responds to us (2 Cor. 1: 3-4).

It is through such compassion that the church establishes a Christian presence. William K. McElvaney indicates that "care is the glue of all Christian ministry," and adds that where there is no caring, there is no Christian presence; and where there is no Christian presence, there is no Christian ministry. (*The People of God in Ministry.* Nashville: Abingdon Press, 1981, p. 144) And Carl S. Dudley says: "I believe that a church is as large as the lives that are touched through the congregation by the love of God. Caring is the ultimate measure of a congregation's size." (*Making the Small Church Effective.* Nashville: Abingdon Press, 1978, pp. 71-72) Our Lord gave us the way of love and compassion. This way is to dominate our nature as a church community. Nothing is more central.

Conclusion

To affirm the congregation as primary caregiver is to acknowledge the significant care which already occurs in the congregation. Social networks, both formal and informal, within the church and the community provide the channels for caregiving relationships. Friendships, fellowship and recreation groups, Bible study and prayer groups, youth groups, women's and men's organizations, and Sunday school classes, all evidence a great deal of the care that occurs in a congregation. In this sense congregational care is often underground and not readily visible.

To promote the congregation as primary caregiver is not an attempt to fit still another program into a busy weekly schedule. Rather, caregiving is an affirmation of the congregation's basic function, divinely designed to bring wholeness to individuals, to the body itself, and to the world.

The Caregiving Team

Al Dueck

Pastoral care in the congregation is the combined result of covenantal relationships between individuals and God, spouses, friends, and strangers. The following is an attempt to develop a model of covenant care in the congregation. There are four types of individuals involved: informal laypersons; formally elected laypersons, including deacons; pastors; and professionals.

I. Informal Caregivers

Carl and Annette have been part of a small group in their congregation for the past fifteen years. It began with two couples and expanded to three couples, a single parent, and two single individuals. They represent different ages and occupations. At first they met simply to be together, play games, and converse. Later one individual suggested they occasionally meet for focused Bible Study. Crisis times have been part of their experience. Two individuals lost a parent through death and one member has developed a slow degenerative disease. During the time of grieving, they supported one another. The group has helped the disabled individual financially and emotionally.

This is an example of one covenant network in a congregation. Sometimes the covenant network is less structured than the group just described and includes such things as telephone contacts, prayer chain, quilting parties, meals after a hospitalization, spontaneous encouragement, gentle rebuke, birthday and retirement parties. Such networks help people meet basic needs of life: friendship, support in crisis, a sense of belonging. These contacts are usually self-initiated in nature. They require few skills and little training, yet they powerfully incarnate God's covenant faithfulness.

Is this pastoral care? Certainly. If such a natural network did not exist, the pastoral counselor, the pastor, and the deacons would have spent much more time in ministering to persons in Carl's and Annette's group.

Pastors and deacons in the congregation can rejoice that these informal networks exist and they can encourage their continuance and effectiveness by being supporting and affirming of the care that is given. They can guard against the church imposing on these groups excessive organization or service tasks that may divert valuable energy away from their care to one another. When pastors and deacons are trusted, they can helpfully guide such groups in their caregiving.

II. Lay/Formal Caregivers

Ruth is a widow in her late fifties. She has worked in the county court as a clerk for more than twenty years. People with needs tend to gravitate to her. Last year Ruth was elected a deacon in her congregation. The council gave her a specific task: develop a support group for recent widows and widowers in the congregation. She began visiting individuals when she heard of a death in the family. Ruth tends to be quiet and listen. She offers little advice, but people know she understands. She was given some help in organizing the group and they meet regularly now.

Informal networks do not ensure that the needs of everyone in the congregation will be met. In the New Testament community the Greek widows were overlooked (Acts 6). Traditionally, deacons responded to the needs of the poor. In addition, the pastor often needs assistance in the general oversight of the congregation, with specific congregational events (baptism, communion, the worship service), in the teaching ministry (premarital counseling, marriage counseling, baptismal classes), in discipling new converts, and in the ministry of encouragement to the sick, the bereaved, and the elderly. The oversight and leading of small caring groups may also be the deacons' responsibility, but these will supplement, not supplant, the self-initiated covenant groups.

Formal training for these lay/formal caregivers is critical in the same way that informal encouragement is critical with the fellowship groups. First, potential deacons need to be aware of the nature of the task, in a way that does not discourage them. Vision needs to be created for the task. This might involve a meeting between potential deacons and several experienced deacons who have made a significant contribution in assisting with pastoral care. The experienced deacons could share what they do and what they have found most difficult and most rewarding.

Next, deacons need to be trained in the specific skills of the office. A workbook could be developed, with clear scenarios of what deacons have experienced, such as conflict between two families, or two businessmen, or a pastor with parishioner. "Student" deacons would respond to the situations and then discuss them with others present. Additional scenarios of actual responses to similar situations could be presented by other deacons.

And, finally, new deacons could be apprentices to experienced deacons, learning "on the job" how to be effective in their work.

III. Ordained/Formal Caregivers

Carol and Kevin co-pastor an older urban congregation. They are very sensitive to the many needs in the congregation. They have spent innumerable hours with those in need but find that their energy is waning. Their creativity in other areas is decreasing. They feel they have neglected each other and their family. They will resign this Sunday.

Carol and Kevin represent the caregiver who has been formally trained and ordained to give full-time, compensated pastoral leadership to a congregation. The degree of competence, experience, training, and self-discipline varies widely among the clergy. Unlike Carol and Kevin some pastors are unaware of the emotional, spiritual, physical, and social needs of the congregation. Then there are pastors who are aware but feel unprepared to handle the complexity or the magnitude of the needs. Some pastors are aware of the need and are immersed in the counseling but find themselves neglecting other responsibilities because of the counseling overload. Happy, of course, is that pastor, and there are some, who is aware of the needs of the congregation and who is also aware of his or her own limitations and does not seek to accomplish the whole pastoral care task alone.

It can be stated with confidence that every pastor can use assistance in discovering and meeting the need for pastoral care in the congregation. This is where the work of trained and committed deacons is so vital. Professional growth for pastors is critical also, to help them develop the skills and confidence required for their unique caregiver role. And every pastor needs a network of other caregiving professionals in the community to whom he or she can make referrals when the counseling load is too heavy or the situation requires more advanced skills and insights.

IV. Trained Counselors/Caregivers

Sharon is a clinical psychologist who has been attending congregational worship services for the past several years after completing graduate studies. Church members are not quite sure how to respond to her since she is a psychologist. The pastor is equally ambivalent, so that when he discovered that physical abuse was a problem in one of the church families, Sharon was not consulted. However, Sharon is eager to be of help. She would be willing to train deacons, see some of the troubled families, or lead a seminar in interpersonal communication.

There are lay persons in many congregations who have special caregiver gifts and training that could be invaluable to the congregation's pastoral ministry. Such persons include medical doctors, psychologists, social workers, marriage and family counselors, nurses, and others. These individuals are often quite willing to share their skills with the church community, given an opportunity to do so.

These trained counselors can be helpful, especially when problems arise within the Christian community that are too complex for the pastoral staff or deacons to handle, such as deep psychological disturbance, incest, or terminal illness. They also can be used effectively to train other caregivers in the church, such as the deacons, in ways of identifying and responding to critical needs of people.

Conclusion

Each of the caregivers listed above plays a very significant role in providing an adequate program of pastoral care for the congregation. It is important that the church recognize the contributions of the informal and professional caregivers as well as those of pastors and deacons. Congregational care demands all the caregivers who are available in the church.

Section Two:
The Role of Deacons in History

A Brief Biblical/ Historical Perspective

Erland Waltner

The position of deacon is as old as the Christian church itself. However, the definition, status, and practice of deacons have been far from consistent as the church has chosen its leaders down through the centuries.

Biblical Background

The central meaning of serving as a deacon, comes directly from the teaching and pattern of Jesus (Mark 9:35; 10:43; John 13:1-20). Jesus is the archetype of the deacon. Therefore, to function as a deacon, in the biblical perspective, is to serve, to minister, to help.

The first New Testament vocabulary includes the verb *diakoneo*, to serve; the noun *diakonia*, the service rendered; and *diakonos*, the one who serves. The development moves from verb to noun. Clearly, the function is more basic than the role or the office.

The basic image of the verb *diakoneo* was to serve as at table, ministering to basic human need. In Greek, this term came to be used of household service more broadly, and then of serving generally, whether in the community or in the larger society.

The vocabulary for service is common and varied in the New Testament. David Schroeder notes how it is used of giving food and drink, providing clothing, visiting the sick or those in prison (Matt. 27:55; 25:42; Mark 15:41), as women and men minister to Jesus and in his name. It is also used of assisting in the preaching of the gospel (Acts 6:4; 19:22; 2 Cor. 11:23). In fact the exercise of any gift (*charisma*) for the benefit of the Christian community to the glory of God is properly described by the same terms (Eph. 4:11f; 1 Cor. 12:4ff; 1 Pet. 4:10). (Schroeder, *Others*, Board of Christian Service, Conference of Mennonites in Canada, 1968, pp 10-11.)

The more specific use of the term *diakonos* to signify a person who has a designated role or "office" in the church appears only in Philippians 1:1 and in 1 Timothy 3:8-12, and probably in Romans 16:1 where it applies to Phoebe. Phoebe is designated not only as *diakonos* (literally, "deacon" rather than "deaconness") but also a *prostatis*, which in secular Greek has a strong connotation of being a leader. This suggests that Phoebe is an early model of the servant-leader in the church of Cenchrea. If this interpretation is correct, the New Testament gives grounds not only for women serving in the church generally but also officially, not only in a subservient role but also in a leadership role. This interpretation, however, is still debated in some congregations. Similarly, 1 Timothy 3:11 remains a controversial passage, which many read as applying to women who are deacons while others read as applying to wives of deacons.

The Pastoral Epistles, in identifying qualifications which Timothy and Titus were to consider in designating leadership in emerging congregations threatened by heresy, focused attention on moral character and faithfulness to the truth of the Gospel rather than on skills. Reputation in the community, relationship to the family, as well as personal disciplines and reliability are noted. Essentially, the qualifications for deacons are not significantly different from those of any other church leader. It is notable that in 1 Timothy, as in Acts 6, special concern about the care of widows finds expression. This introduces, in principle, the importance of mutual aid in the Christian community, in which deacons have a significant role.

Related New Testament vocabulary includes the word *doulos* which means bond-servant or slave but which focuses on the particular relationship between the "slave" and the "master," while *diakonos* generally focuses on concrete ministry to manifest human need. Another term is *hyperetes* which means assistant, or literally "under-rower" as in a galley ship, and carries the image of subservience as in "servants of the word" (Luke 1:2) or "servants of Christ" (1 Cor.4:1).

The tradition that the office of the deacon goes back to Acts 6:1-6 is questioned by some scholars. The "seven" appointed in this passage are not called *diakonos* even though functions identified in this passage speak of "serving tables" (6:3), in view of the particular needs of the neglected widows, and "serving the word" (6:4), considered a particular responsibility of the apostles. However, "the seven," especially Stephen and Philip, did much more than serve tables. They also became active in the proclamation of the Gospel. Philip later is called an evangelist (Acts 21:8). This indicates that ministries in the New Testament were not narrowly defined as belonging to specific roles or offices. The basis for ministry was gift (*chrisma*) rather than a defined church office held (1 Cor. 12:4ff).

Historical Developments

It is not clear when the "office" of deacon emerged. In the New Testament, the basic emphasis is on function, with only the emergence of the notion of office. In postbiblical development, the church clearly recognized three internal offices, perceiving these in a hierarchical perspective: the deacon as the lowest order; the priest/elder as a middle order; and finally, the bishop/overseer as the highest order. This hierarchical order becomes clear in the writings of St. Ignatius of Antioch and Polycarp of Smyrna.

In the further development of the role of deacons in the church, two discernable foci emerge. The first focus follows the Roman Catholic tradition and perceives the deacon primarily in terms of assisting or serving other church leaders, priests, or bishops. The emphasis falls on deacons assisting in the worship services of the church, though not excluding ministries to the sick and the poor. Thus, in Anglicanism "the deacon is to assist at divine service, to read the Scriptures and the homilies, to instruct in the catechism, to baptize and to preach if permitted, to seek out the poor, sick, and infirm, and to help solicit and distribute alms" (*International Standard Bible Encyclopedia*, I:880 Eerdmans, 1979).

The other focus accents the framework of the priesthood of all believers and moves away from hierarchical perspectives. In the Reformed tradition, Calvin focused on the care of the poor and needy and the distribution of alms as the primary role for deacons (Acts 6:1-6). He also assigned deacons to assist elders in serving the Lord's Supper and to encourage the people to commune.

Brethren and Mennonite traditions, though drawing from both streams, have generally found themselves closer to the Reformed than to the Anglican tradition, emphasizing shared ministry rather than hierarchical orders. Anabaptist and later Baptist patterns tended to include a very wide range of functions which deacons might serve. In a Baptist Church Survey in *The Deacon In a Changing Church* (Judson Press, 1969), Donald F. Thomas reported no less than twenty specific functions served by deacons; the most common were assisting in communion services, assisting at baptism, providing for pulpit ministry, calling on the sick and shut-ins, and administering a deacons' fund for the needy poor.

Guy F. Hershberger of Goshen, Indiana, makes a strong plea that deacons should become more active pastoral care providers and channels of congregational mutual aid. He identifies such functions as pastoral care of a designated group of members, leadership in fellowship groups, more pastoral visitation, leading in responding to crises, stimulating spontaneous mutual aid, responding to the needs of the aging, the special needs of youth, the newly married, families in trouble, giving counsel in business/ professional ethics, on neighborhood ethical issues, promoting voluntary service, leading in the discipling of members. (Hershberger, "The Congregation and Its Need for a Diaconate in a Changing Era," unpublished, 1966.)

In both Church of the Brethren and Mennonite congregations the role of deacon in recent years has experienced change in nature and status. In the late 19th century and the first four decades of this century, the office of deacon wielded much power in many congregations. Part of this influence was due to the annual diaconal visit which could result in the disciplining of members and their exclusion from communion services. When the deacon visit became too anxiety-producing, congregations began to drop the practice; this, in turn, lessened both the responsibilities and the authority of deacons.

In other congregations, the deacons themselves simply took a less visible and less active role in the life of the congregation. Factors which contributed to this less active role included the rise of salaried pastors and the impact of greater cultural diversions such as television and a more urbanized environment. Then, the office of deacon declined in influence as well as in activity, and gradually began to give way to other patterns of ministry and leadership.

In recent years, in response to a sense of loss when diaconal leadership declined, the role and office of the deacon are being renewed. The publication of this resource is itself a response to this situation and a part of this process.

Conclusion

Biblically and historically, to serve as a deacon is a high and holy calling, never to be entered upon lightly, but always in the fear of God, looking to Jesus Christ as pattern, and guided and empowered by the Holy Spirit working in the fellowship of the believing congregation.

Variations in Anabaptist Traditions

Harold E. Bauman

Erland Waltner reports that the various Anabaptist traditions have generally followed the Reformed tradition in understanding the work and status of deacons. Deacons have been responsible for the care of the poor and needy, assisting in administering the ordinances, and assisting in the worship service. This is in contrast to the Anglican tradition where the deacon is viewed as an ordained minister immediately below the rank of priest. During some periods in our history, however, the concept of deacons in some Anabaptist groups has come very close to the Anglican view.

There are variations in how the ministry and status of deacons have been expressed in the Anabaptist traditions. In understanding the variations, it is important to view the work and status of deacons in relation to the work and status of other congregational leaders.

Changing Leadership Patterns

Generally, all the denominations cooperating in this resource had what is called a "free ministry," where persons were called from the congregation and ordained to the ministry. They earned their own livelihood and, in addition, served the congregation.

The change to a trained and salaried ministry in the General Conference Mennonite Church and the Mennonite Brethren Church came first in congregations in the United States. The change has come more slowly in the Canadian congregations. The Church of the Brethren has experienced a similar change, beginning the first part of the twentieth century and gradually increasing.

The change to a trained salaried ministry in the Mennonite Church has come more recently. Some conferences made the change largely 20 to 30 years ago. In other conferences the change has been more recent. Some conferences have a variety of leadership patterns: some ministers who are trained and salaried full-time and some who are bivocational and serve part-time or on marginal time.

The Brethren in Christ had leadership patterns similar to the early stages of the Mennonite Church and the Church of the Brethren. Since 1940 there has been movement to a trained and salaried leadership among the Brethren in Christ.

Spiritual Oversight and Management

Before looking at patterns of leadership which have emerged, we need to look at a major shift in the primary focus of congregational leadership. This has come about in part with the proliferation of many activities and programs in congregational life. There needs to be *management* of activities, as well as preparation for preaching and crisis visitation. The focus on management of activities often moves to the front, while concerns for the spiritual oversight of the congregation may receive minimal time.

What did the leadership formerly do? They generally had the primary focus on spiritual oversight. Let me set this in the context of spiritual oversight provided in the New Testament as seen in Acts and the epistles. Oversight of the life and mission of the congregation involved:

1. Discerning the spiritual needs in the body and helping the congregation develop and keep in focus the vision of its life and mission.
2. Overseeing the ministry in Word and worship, modeling and providing preaching, overseeing the preaching needs, and training others in worship leading and preaching.
3. Overseeing and participating in the equipping of church members for the use of their spiritual gifts in ministry within and beyond the congregation.
4. Overseeing and modeling mutual care—the priesthood of all believers—and seeing that every member has a primary place for giving and receiving such care; and overseeing and providing crisis pastoral care.
5. Facilitating decision-making in the congregation on leadership selection and policy issues.

Earlier leadership groups of the five denominations sponsoring this resource were concerned about the quality and direction of the faith and life of the congregation. They dealt with the above areas in spiritual oversight. The change in leadership patterns has tended to turn over the first four items to the pastor, especially the preaching and pastoral care, and the last item to an *ex officio* group. The large additional function is the need for management of activities.

Leadership Patterns which Emerged

With the change to a salaried full-time ministry, several leadership patterns have emerged. One pattern is to call a trained pastor as the primary person who does ministry for the congregation. The pastor generally works with an executive committee or a church council consisting of *ex officio* persons (chairpersons of the various committees). Many such groups spend most of their time overseeing the activities of the congregation, a management function. Many pastors experience being left with the responsibility for spiritual oversight of the congregation, a very lonely walk.

A second pattern continues the plural leadership heritage and includes the resource of a trained person. While the trained person is often salaried, the other members of the spiritual oversight team serve on marginal time.

The management of activities is usually done by another leadership group, (church council, cabinet, or board) with the pastor and the chairperson of the spiritual oversight group providing liaison between the two groups. Thus spiritual oversight is given by a leadership group chosen for that task and not by *ex officio* persons chosen for other tasks.

Overview of Denominational Patterns

The place and work of deacons in these two patterns has varied considerably in our denominations.

In the Church of the Brethren, there are two leadership patterns. Each may have some variations from one congregation to another. One pattern is to have eight to twelve committees. The chairpersons along with the pastor make up the church board. One of the committees usually is a board of deacons. There may also be a ministry committee which works with the pastor in ministerial relations and in some instances in the spiritual oversight of the congregation.

In a second leadership pattern in the Church of the Brethren, the congregation elects a church board which divides itself into three to seven commissions. The chairpersons of the commissions along with the pastor and several church officers make up an executive committee which gives leadership to the congregation. There is also a deacon body which is separate from the church board. The chairperson of the deacons may serve on the executive committee.

There is presently in the Church of the Brethren a renewed vision to restore the office of deacon (the term used for both women and men who serve in the office). Deacons are to assist in the preparation and administering of the ordinances and Love Feast, minister to the poor and needy, assist in ministry to the sick and shut-ins and bereaved, provide a ministry of reconciliation and restoration, and develop a shepherding program in the congregation in cooperation with the pastor.

Among Brethren in Christ congregations there is considerable variety in regard to patterns of deacon ministry. Many congregations have a pastor serving with a church council, with deacons as part of the council. Other congregations have deacons whose main function is to aid in the observance of the ordinances. Some add the work of caring for the poor and needy. Some congregations are assigning to the deacons the work of undershepherds, a task similar to that recommended for deacons in the Church of the Brethren.

In the Mennonite Brethren Church, deacons have been a part of congregational ministry and have been ordained for life. With the coming of the paid minister, there is no uniform pattern in regard to deacons. Generally there is an *ex officio* church council with whom the pastor works. There are few boards of elders. The diaconate is continued but the deacons are not ordained for life as was done formerly. Deacons help with the ordinances, oversee the care of the needy, and in some congregations are in charge of care groups.

Deacons in the General Conference Mennonite Church have served in the care of the poor and needy. In many congregations they have also assisted the pastor in the spiritual oversight of the congregation, thus forming a plural leadership group. A church council provides for the coordination of congregational activities.

In the Mennonite Church, historically, along with the ministers and bishops, deacons have been a part of the "three-fold" ministry. Deacons looked after the poor, assisted with the ordinances, assisted in the worship services as needed, and worked at reconciliation among members. With the coming of trained pastors who generally led the worship and did the pastoral care of members, and with the increased affluence in the economy since World War II, the need for deacons appeared to have diminished. As deacons retired, many congregations did not replace them; so now many congregations do not have deacons.

However, several shifts in leadership patterns in the Mennonite Church appear to be taking place. One shift is that many congregations which moved from a plural ministry to a trained pastor working solo are now returning to plural leadership for spiritual oversight of the congregation. Most frequently this takes the form of choosing three or more elders (depending upon the size of the congregation) to serve with the pastor in spiritual oversight. The elders also usually assist in leading worship and in the observance of the ordinances. In some congregations they are responsible for the care of the poor and needy.

The second shift is to reconsider restoring the office of deacon. With the increased number of persons in congregations needing financial assistance in view of the changing economy, more time and special skills are needed to look after these needs. In addition, there is a growing vision of the work of elders with the pastor in the spiritual oversight of the congregation. Their work takes all the time that persons serving on marginal time can give without adding the work of deacons.

Thus, there is a new look at the work of deacons in the Mennonite Church. Some congregations are returning to calling deacons who deal with financial needs of members and assist with the ordinances. Some may be called for a specified term and are commissioned to their work. Others may be called for a specified term and are ordained for as long as they carry the responsibilities. A few may be ordained for life. Some deacons also serve in the spiritual oversight group.

To complete the picture of the leadership patterns of our denominations, we need to note that there have also been persons who gave oversight between several or more congregations. These persons were called bishops (Brethren in Christ and Mennonite Church) or elders (the other three groups). Some denominations continue to use bishops or overseers, while others have district executives or conference ministers. The chart below includes these persons for the nineteenth century, but does not include them for the current situation because the focus is on the internal leadership of the congregation.

Summary

The task of the church is to be a priesthood of believers who minister to each other and to those outside the community of faith. The community of faith needs a leadership group to give spiritual oversight and to equip the members for their ministry. Since congregations also have many programs and activities, there also needs to be a management group whose function is program coordination. There is also a need for persons who look after the poor and needy and who help with the ordinances.

A view of the above history is presented here in chart form. The chart shows those persons working in spiritual oversight during the nineteenth and early twentieth centuries. It then moves to the present scene (currently), showing both the spiritual oversight group and the management group. In the present scene, when deacons are functioning but not generally as part of the spiritual oversight group they are indicated as (Deacons).

The Congregation:
Priests in Mutual and Outreach Ministries

The Congregation is enabled in this ministry by:	19th and early 20th century / Currently	Brethren in Christ Church	Church of the Brethren	Gen. Conf. Mennonite Church	Mennonite Brethren Church	Mennonite Church
A Spiritual Oversight Group	19th and early 20th century	Bishop Ministers Deacons	Elders Ministers Deacons	Elders Ministers Deacons	Elders Ministers Deacons	Bishops Ministers Deacons
A Spiritual Oversight Group *and*	Currently	Pastor (Deacons)	Pastor (Deacons)	Pastor Deacons	Pastor (Deacons)	Pastor Elders Deacons
A Management Group		Church Council	Church Board	Church Council	Church Council	Church Council

One needs to note the different use of the term "elder" in the Church of the Brethren, the General Conference Mennonite Church, and the Mennonite Brethren Church in the nineteenth century in comparison with the Mennonite Church today. Also note that the office of elder in the Mennonite Church shares in the work of spiritual oversight as do the deacons in the General Conference Mennonite Church; generally, however, elders do not share all of the work historically given to deacons.

Thus, when this resource speaks of the work of deacons, persons in each denomination will need to do some adapting to their setting.

Remembering How It Was: An Interview with John Lapp and Clarence Kulp

June A. Gibble

June: The word deacon has some differences of meaning in our denominations, or perhaps the meaning has changed over the years. So first I would like to ask you, John, what the word deacon means in Mennonite groups.

John: We usually think of the deacon as the treasurer of the congregation, the one responsible for ministering to the needs of the poor according to the gifts of the church and the needs of individual members. I am more familiar with the Mennonite Church in America than its background in Europe. In Germantown the first preacher was William Rittenhouse and the first deacon was Jan Nice; in 1698, they were chosen by the congregation to fill these offices. So far as I know Nice continued as the deacon throughout the span of his life.

The purpose of deacons at that time was to care for the needs of the poor and there were many poor people. When the Mennonites came to America, the Mennonites of Europe sometimes gave them money for their passage; and they would tell them to put this in the poor fund of their congregation when they were able: "We have helped you, now you help someone else." And then gradually deacons became a more powerful force in congregational life; I don't know why it happened, but it did. The common name by which deacons were known in Pennsylvania German was *vorsteher*, the one who presides in the congregation." Why deacons were given the name *vorsteher*, I don't know. I know we, as young people, used to say it meant the one who stands up front, a front-stander. But, simply put, the deacon is the mutual aid treasurer of the congregation.

June: Thank you, John. And now, Clarence, what about the meaning of the word deacon for the Church of the Brethren over the years?

Clarence: Certainly the Church of the Brethren shares with the Mennonites the interpretation of the deacon as one who is concerned with the physical needs of the brothers and sisters. There were occasions in early periods and in the 19th century when the Brethren used the same term for deacon that is used today by old order Amish people—the term *armendiener* or "servant of the poor." In the early period of the Church of the Brethren we have very little information on deacons, who deacons were, whether the deacon office was an office that initiated at the beginning of the Church of the Brethren, or whether it was initiated slightly later. The earliest sources I know do seem to indicate that the original function was being a servant to the poor, taking care of the poor, first in the congregation and also the poor of the community.

The first reference we have to a Brethren deacon is found in the tradition of the Church of the Brethren in Holland, when Alexander Mack and his group were journeying in Friesland. In his journal Mack mentions a dear brother, and I believe he used the term *almosen-pfleger* which means one who takes care of the alms. He says this dear brother in the church at Friesland was a wealthy man who apparently had been in politics; he took the office of deacon so seriously that he gave to the poor from his own fortune 50,000 guilders annually. That was a very great gift.

Later, perhaps because of Mennonite influence, Brethren deacons assumed a disciplinary function; how far back the idea of visiting brethren goes we're not sure, but certainly by the early 19th century a deacon was *bsuch bruder*, a visiting brother who came to take the spiritual temperature of the congregation just prior to *Liebesmahl* (Love Feast).

June: Thank you, Clarence. And now, John, I want to check about one more thing. In the Mennonite church today, do elders assume some of the functions that once belonged to the deacons?

John: Yes, there are elders in a number of congregations, and some congregations do not want to choose a deacon. They would rather use their elders to perform the work of the deacon; then the congregational treasurer is the one who issues the checks. But this is not true in all congregations; even some congregations who have no ordained deacon do have elected deacons or a deacon committee. And let me also say . . . I don't know that I ever heard the German term *armen-diener* in Mennonite circles. I have heard the term *almsloser*; as a boy, I heard our German preaching bishop talk about *almsloser* sometimes.

June: Thank you. Now I am interested in knowing whether the deacon office is actually as old as our denominations. What do we know about the beginning of the office of deacon, John?

John: Well, the Mennonite church has always considered the work of the deacon and the care of the poor to be more important than the names of members who were baptized. We have deacon records that go way back; the Skippack record goes back to about 1720. And yet we don't know the names of the people who were baptized in those days; they kept no record of it. The point is, the care of the poor was more important than how many numbers we could add to the congregations.

June: That is special to know. Clarence, the same question. Were there deacons at the very beginning of the Church of the Brethren?

Clarence: We simply don't know. I don't know of any listing of deacons at the very beginning or in the first several years. The earliest reference to a deacon in the Church of the Brethren would be . . . his name comes to me now . . . the name is Adrian Pfau, the wealthy Hollander, who became

Brethren and then served the church by dispersing the church's money to the poor and also dispersing from his own fortune.

From records of early Colonial America Brethren, it seems that for almost the first century of the Church of the Brethren the deacon office was primarily concerned with caring for the physical needs of the poor— reflecting their interpretation that the original deacons were chosen to wait on the physical needs of people. We also have in the Church of the Brethren some very early colonial alms records; these are fascinating records of how monies were collected and dispersed through the office of deacon in the 18th and early 19th centuries.

June: So apparently, in both Mennonite and Brethren traditions, the care of the poor and giving of alms was an important part of the earliest deacon functions. Now I am interested in the calling of deacons. John, you mentioned the first deacon chosen in Germantown, in the Mennonite church. Do we know how these early deacons were called to their office?

John: I think the congregation agreed that these persons should be the ones who should serve. Historically, traditionally, in America and I think in Europe also, all of the officers of the church were chosen by the congregations, and by the casting of lots if there was more than one person named by the congregation. The lot was used until about 1960 here in Franconia conference. Usually one deacon is chosen for smaller or average-size congregations, and two deacons for the larger congregations. Traditionally, Franconia had two deacons, Blooming Glen had two deacons, and Deep Run had two deacons. They were the three larger congregations in the conference.

June: So, the calling of deacons was by lot.

John: Yes, and ministers and bishops were chosen that way, also. I was chosen by lot in 1933 and in 1937 again. When I was ordained preacher, at Plains, six of us shared the lot; and when I was chosen bishop at Franconia, there were six ministers again.

Clarence: In the early periods, historically, in both the Church of the Brethren and the Mennonite Church, deacons were not ordained by the laying on of hands, nor were preachers—only bishops. Occasionally a deacon was ordained in smaller congregations where there was no bishop or preacher; then one of the deacons would be chosen as the administrative head of the congregation and they would ordain the deacon by laying on of hands. He then became a confirmed or ordained deacon. So ordination has gone through a great transition in both the Mennonite Church and the Church of the Brethren through the last two centuries. In more recent times, we have ordained our preachers and also our deacons by laying on of hands. But that's not the old way.

John: I'd like to add a word about the deacon office being considered so important. In the Mennonite church here in Franconia conference, when a new congregation was formed, the first office to be filled was that of a deacon. The Plains church was organized between 1760 and 1769 ... we usually say 1765. The first preacher, John Krupp, was chosen in 1816. There was a deacon by the name of John Weyerman very much earlier. We don't have the date of his ordination or of his being called as deacon, but he signed the audits in 1779. So for 37 years there was no preacher chosen for the congregation, but there was a deacon. Then the Souderton congregation was formed about 1879; Henry Krupp was chosen as the first deacon in 1891 and Jacob M. Moyer was chosen as the first preacher in 1912. So in the first years there was no preacher but there was a deacon, and a very active deacon.

June: That certainly indicates the importance of deacons in the earliest congregations.

John: Henry Krupp kept careful records of his deacon work. He had records where he had paid a family to keep a man in their home; and he went to the store and bought this man a shirt and trousers; he has the cost in his deacon book. He was careful about keeping all those records.

Clarence: It is also true in the Church of the Brethren that our deacon records, the alms records, go much farther back than any other. In the Indian Creek Church, my congregation, the records of congregational decisions go back to the turn of the last century; but financial records, deacon records, go back almost a century earlier. So, in the Mennonite Church in the 19th and early 20th centuries and to a somewhat lesser degree in the Church of the Brethren, I would say that the office of deacon was the one congregational office which was considered indispensable.

June: We've clearly moved into the 19th century now. Is there anything else about the 19th century office of deacon that you want to share with us?

John: In the Mennonite Church I don't know of anyone who was chosen for deacon who refused to fill the office. I think everybody considered that what the deacons were doing was so important; that's why they were respected and given authority in the congregation. That's why they were given disciplinary authority. Deacons were usually men who couldn't speak too much in public but they were able to talk to people in private and say a word that would be very helpful. For instance, Vincent Bergey was a deacon in the Franconia congregation. He and I went to visit in a home one day; a lady showed us a book and said, "We build very much on this book." I tried to point out a few questionable things in that book, but Vincent Bergey said more than I did in all of my talking. He pointed to the Bible and said, "Here's the book you can use with safety, you can depend on this."

Clarence: It's interesting . . . from the records and also from talking to older people, the feeling I get is that the office of deacon in the 19th century was considered more important than the office of minister. On a scale of importance, the bishop would be on the top, then the deacon, and then the minister.

John: Yes. An interesting sidelight here. About 1936 before I was chosen as a bishop, J. C. Clemens, the Secretary of the conference, and I were on our way to conference. He said, "Yesterday the bishops were having a discussion and one of them said, 'If we move in this direction, we'll subject ourselves to discipline.' Another bishop asked, 'Who will discipline the bishops?' The immediate answer came, 'The deacons will.' "

June: That illustrates what I'm hearing you both say, that the office of deacon, beginning as those who were the alms givers, caring for the needs of the poor, moved gradually to include a more authoritarian function.

Clarence: Definitely. In the Mennonite Church it became very authoritarian for a time. And at the same time it was becoming more authoritarian, it was paying more attention to the spiritual temperature of the congregation and individuals. The office of deacon became sort of an arm of the office of bishop, because bishops were involved in administering and disciplining. Ministers were mainly thought of in the role of preaching, but deacons visited, they had the more intimate contact.

June: Was this true in Brethren churches as well as Mennonite?

Clarence: To a lesser degree. I am thinking now of the Mennonite church. In the Mennonite Church deacons would come into your home to discipline or to bring alms or needed supplies. I can remember as a boy when we had several Mennonites working for us. I believe at least two of them were under some sort of discipline of the Mennonite church. The deacons came to visit our hired men during the day; they asked my father to give the men a little time off so they could talk. They sat in an automobile for a long time, I remember, in earnest conversation and praying. I got a sense growing up that the Mennonite deacon was to be respected.

John: I think it was the authoritarian attitude of some deacons that put them into disrepute, so that the congregations no longer wanted to have deacons. I think that's why they decided to settle for elders.

June: I'd like to ask, Clarence, about the Annual Visit of the Church of the Brethren. I know that has been important in our history. What can you tell us about the Annual Visit, including some childhood memories?

Clarence: I don't know if we have records to show when the Annual Visit first began in the German Baptist or Brethren groups, but we do have evidence from Annual Meeting minutes that it was considered important as far back as the early 19th century. At some point in the Brethren tradition, the term for deacon that became dominate was the German term *bsuch bruder* or visiting brother. It was usually spoken of in the plural, *bsuch brieder* or visiting brethren. Very early in the Church of the Brethren the function of performing the Annual Visit became even more important than the function of dispersing alms.

The Annual Visit, the *Jahrlich Bsuch*, was conducted every year before Love Feast and communion; generally in the 19th and 20th century, Brethren had Love Feast once a year. In our congregation that was in the spring, usually around Pentecost. Prior to that, a month or six weeks before, the deacons would pair up two by two. If there weren't enough deacons, a minister would pair up with a deacon to go out for the Annual Visit but I don't ever remember two preachers going. If a preacher went, he went with a deacon because the deacon was the visiting brother.

Then in the middle of the 20th century many congregations began to dispense with the Annual Visit. This was a part of the decline of the deacon office in the Church of the Brethren . . . and also the decline of the concept of discipling one another. Permit a personal reflection: We gave up the Annual Visit probably at a time when we needed it most; because of the general decline of the concept of community and *gemeinschaft* among our people, we needed that contact.

I can best illustrate the importance and the meaning of the Annual Visit by speaking from my own experience. I remember when I was a boy growing up, before I was baptized and also afterward, how important and how exciting an event the deacon visit was. I remember quite clearly my father's country general store; the store would be open late six evenings a week because a lot of people did their shopping in the evening. Every evening the local farmers and townspeople would come in and sit around the potbellied stove, exchange stories and folk tales, and rehearse the news of the day or the week.

I remember how my father would say during the day or perhaps early in the evening to me and to my mother *"Den owet komme die bsuch brieders."* "This evening the visiting brethren are coming." I remember how I anticipated that and how exciting it was to me. I would think about it all afternoon and then in the evening I would look out the front windows, and my mother would look out the window, and "Are they here yet? Is that their car coming in?" Then we would see them getting out of the car and coming up over the porch. Our house had two front doors, one into the general store and the other into the parlor. Of course, they would head for the door that went into the parlor. Then my father would turn over the reins to one of the store sitters and he would say, *"De bsuch brider sin do."* "The visiting brethren are here . . . and we will have to go over into the parlor for a while."

Then my father, my mother, and I would go into the parlor; my father would open the door and the visiting brethren would come in. They would greet my father with a holy kiss, shake hands with my mother, and shake hands with me. They always made me feel important for some reason. We would sit down and they would begin simply visiting like neighbors who were just enjoying a good visit; for 10 or 15 minutes or perhaps sometimes longer we would talk about the weather, the price of hogs and cattle, who just got married or had a baby, who was sick and who had died.

And then, I remember, all of a sudden, everything got sorta still and usually the older of the two would say, "Now brother and sister, we have come here on very important business." And his voice would change to a much more solemn and sort of ecclesiastical tone and he would say, "I suppose you know the reason we have come; we have a few questions that the church asks us to ask you." By this time, I was really excited.

I remember how usually the older brother would ask, "Are you still in the faith as you were when you came into the church by baptism?" He would turn to my father, and my father would quietly say "yes" and nod his head;

and then to my mother; and later on, when I was a member, to me. Then the second question, "Are you willing to work on with the congregation of the church of Christ at this place?" And my father would say "yes" and my mother. Then the most important question, "Are you, as far as it lies with you, living at peace with all men?" My father would say "yes," and my mother would say "yes." Finally they would say, "Now if you have any matters to be brought before the council meeting in a week or two, something you feel the church is in need of, or some spiritual counsel, we will carry it." And sometimes my father or my mother would have something to say.

It was quiet for a while. Then they would ask my father, "If you will permit it, we will engage in a season of prayer before we leave." We all knelt down in the parlor there and usually both of them prayed; then we got up and they would again give the holy kiss and leave. Looking back on it, I see that it was probably the most intimate contact our family had with the church at any time. That I see as the peculiar quality and ability that is invested in the deacon office . . . that intimate brotherly, sisterly connection. I think that's why we need the office of deacon because that is the genius of the deacon office in the church.

June: Thanks for sharing your story with us, Clarence. And now I want to ask one other question about the function of deacons. What do the deacons do in the worship life of the church or in other special forms of church life?

John: In the Mennonite church the deacons would read the scripture in the opening of the service. Some deacons would lead the congregation in prayer audibly. After the sermon and before the closing prayer, we had a time of testimony; then the preacher, if there was one besides the one who delivered the sermon, and the deacon would both be expected to give a testimony. Jim Gerhardt tells a story about a deacon at Swamp church. This particular deacon was in the habit of sleeping every Sunday morning during the sermon. Then when it came time for testimony he would be awake, and he would say, "I can say Amen to everything I heard in the service."

June: Well, Clarence, how about the deacons in Brethren worship?

Clarence: Their function in worship in the Church of the Brethren would be very similar to the Mennonite church. Traditionally in the German Baptist or Brethren groups you would have a preachers' table. The bishops or elders and the preachers would sit behind the table facing the congregation; the deacons would sit opposite them on the deacons' bench, facing the preachers and with their backs to the congregation.

In my growing up years, the deacon in our congregation always read the scripture lessons; this was what we always called the rotation chapter. We went through the New Testament, beginning with the first chapter of Matthew—some Brethren congregations didn't go through the book of Revelation and others did—then we began at the beginning again. That was called *'s capittel in die roi*, "the chapter in the row" or the rotation chapter.

The deacon would always read that. Also in Brethren services, after the sermon or sermons, any preachers who hadn't spoken or any deacons would have the opportunity to testify or bear witness to what had been said. They would usually begin by saying in Pennsylvania Dutch, *"Ich kann ya und amen sage zu die lehr de liebe brieder."* "I can say yea and amen to the doctrine or teaching of our beloved brethren." Some would also say, "Our brethren have spoken so well on this subject that there is really nothing that can possibly be added but . . . " and then they would go on for another 15-20 minutes!

June: I have a concluding question now. John, you mentioned the decline in the office of deacon in Mennonite churches. What changes or transitions are taking place in the office and functions of deacons in our denominations?

John: Well, I think one of the reasons for the decline in the office was the more authoritarian attitude of deacons in more recent history. The second reason was that some deacons thought they had hardly anything to do since Social Security; and the third reason was because some women felt that we should have deaconesses in the church as well and some congregations would not be ready for that. It seems to me it would be in harmony with the 1632 Dordrecht Confession of faith to include deaconnesses with deacons, to have several persons serving as a team; this could be couples or it could be other than couples. There are unmarried women or widows who are very capable for this kind of work and they could well serve with some deacons in the congregation.

June: Thank you, John. And, Clarence, in the Church of the Brethren what changes are occurring?

Clarence: I think there has been a general decline in the last several decades. In our own congregation I have seen the office of deacon go from an order in the ministry (the deacon was always considered a minister) to what it is today, just a sub-committee under the Nurture Commission. I think the decline can probably be attributed to the fact that the functions have been disappearing. The peculiar work of deacons was to administer the functions of the community, the brotherhood-base style of congregation. In the last several decades we have opted for Social Security and old age pensions and retirement homes, and that has erased a deacon function. We have gone from a brotherhood style church to a structured, individualistic sort of bureaucratic structure and that has taken away the deacon visit, the one-to-one ministry. Also we have decided that individuals do what their interpretation leads them to do, and that has erased the disciplinary function of deacons.

I see the value of the deacon office today in revitalizing that intimate brotherhood ministry, not preached from the pulpit, but the one-to-one, brethren and sisters coming together in the home, the ministry on the intimate level.

June: Well, thanks to both of you for sharing with us. During this interview we have heard how the office of deacon has been experienced as a very significant ministry in the life of our people. And at this point in time we are in the midst of transition and change, seeking new light and understandings. And now, Clarence and John, is there a concluding statement you might like to give?

Clarence: I think it would be that the office of deacon was a part of the ministry. I would emphasize that, both in the Church of the Brethren and in the Mennonite Church, the deacon was a minister, a minister on the brotherhood level, on the community intimate level. That is the value of the office. I am bothered when I see this important office of ministry becoming a sub-committee. Deacons should again be ministers.

John: I would say "Amen" to what Clarence has said. And I would recommend that the office be given a bit of new life and new spark, that this important office of deacon be revitalized.

Section Three:
Reclaiming the Office of Deacon

The Image and Ministry of Deacons Within the Congregation

Fred W. Swartz

Pastor Jones recognized Hazel's voice as soon as he answered the telephone. He noted a bit of tentativeness as she asked if he had enjoyed his week of vacation.

"You know how vacations are," he responded, "you begin to get spoiled just as it's time to go back to work." Not picking up on his observation, Hazel moved to the reason for her call. "While you were away Rita called me. Pastor, she talked a long time about problems in her family. She said she called *me* because I was a deacon and she knew I would understand and would pray for her. I've been over to see her twice since then. She would like a visit from you as soon as it's convenient. You know, responding to Rita has helped me see how important this caring ministry of the deacons can be for the life of our church."

Pastor Hewitt was concentrating on point two of his sermon for Sunday when the shrill ring of the telephone shattered his thought progression. "Reverend!" boomed the attention-demanding tone of Arthur Tonket, one of the congregation's lifetime deacons, alias self-appointed ruling elders. "I want this talk about building an addition to the church stopped right now! I've heard that the executive committee has made an appointment with an architect without consulting the deacons as to whether we should even spend our money on more unused space. When I see this church filled to overflowing every Sunday, then it will be time to talk about expanding. You're going to have trouble, preacher, if you don't work with the deacons on this!"

As they say in the theater, the above situations "are true; only the names have been changed to protect the innocent" (or the writer!). We find in these two situations two very different but very real and current perceptions of the role of the deacon within the life of the congregation. In the first, the deacon was seen as one who would care enough about another person to understand . . . and to pray; very much like a pastoral role. In the second, the deacon perceived himself, at least, as having authority over—indeed, one who "called the shots" about—what the church did or didn't do.

The profile of the deacon in the New Testament church seems to match more closely the first of our perceptions—that of the caring servant. In fact,

Thomas Lindsey in his book *The Church and the Ministry in the Early Centuries* (New York: George H. Doran Company, n.d.) states that there were two types of leaders in the first Christian parish—"the serving and the leading . . . the *diaconien* (deacons) and the *episcopein* (overseers). . . ." To the first were given the responsibilities of seeing that spiritual and physical needs of the people were cared for; to the overseers were given the tasks of providing for the assembling and the activities of the Christian fellowship (c.f. Acts 6:1-7).

Deacons can be most effective and valuable to the life and mission of the congregation only as they and the rest of the congregation perceive them as ministers, not managers, of the church program. This wholesome function can be achieved if deacons are selected and regarded as set-apart leaders, as servants, as examples, and as witnesses.

Set-apart. Both the call and the commission of a deacon are unlike that of any other lay leaders in the church. The most important qualification for the office of deacon is demonstration of spiritual commitment and faithfulness (1 Tim. 3:8-13). Deacons are not selected to perform some particular administrative task in the church program, such as financial secretary, food closet manager, or church school superintendent.

The church, therefore, should select its deacons with much seriousness and preparation, in much the same way it calls its ordained ministers. While all members of the congregation are in a sense "ministers" to one another (1 Pet. 2:9), the early church found it helpful to set apart several of its most gifted people to make certain that the serving love of Christ was administered in an intentional, orderly fashion.

The significance of the deacon's qualifications and task suggests that the selection of a deacon be made with much sensitivity and prayer. Although scripture does not reveal how the first deacons were chosen, it makes sense that deacons are more appropriately "called" than "elected." Whether candidates are proposed by a nominating committee or by an open floor procedure, the process should be preceded by study of the biblical models and by much prayer for the leading of the Spirit. When persons are discovered who "meet" the standards of spiritual leadership, those persons should be affirmed by the congregation and considered set-apart ministers. There is no need for an election process in the sense of "choosing the best person for the job." Further, although the setting of terms for deacons is helpful for periodic review and evaluation, a call to a deacon should be considered indefinite, so long as the deacon remains qualified and does not choose to give up the office.

Servants. It is important to establish the concept within the congregation that the primary reason for the existence of deacons is service. The biblical model is found in the self-proclamation of Jesus' own role, as one who "came not to be served, but to serve" (Mark 10:45). Jesus was explicit in describing the role of those who could minister in his name: "Whoever would be great among you, let that one be your servant . . . " (Matt. 20:26).

Deacons are servants of the church. Thirty-five years ago, shortly after the body of deacons in congregations began to be referred to as the deacon *board*, Gaines S. Robbins, a former professor of church administration at Southern Baptist Theological Seminary in Louisville, issued a warning. In his book, *The Church-book* (Nashville: Broadman Press, 1951), he said, "The objection to this designation ("deacon *board*") is that it may somehow imply that deacons are managers rather than ministrants. Deacons are not to give orders to the church; they are to receive instructions from the church. . . . They should never arrogate to themselves any authority for running the church. Their greatest service to the church will usually be found in their assistance to the pastor . . ." (pp. 65-66).

The servant ministry of the deacon body can be very effective when coordinated through a shepherding program. By specifically assigning responsibility for a small group of the church's fellowship to individual or teams of deacons, it is assured that someone besides the pastor is concerned about the ongoing spiritual and physical needs of every individual.

Examples. The congregation should call to the office of deacon those persons whose commitment and faithfulness have been proven in relationship to the local fellowship of believers. Deacons thus can be looked to as persons who lead exemplary lives in loyalty to the church and in love and ministry to others. This is not to imply that deacons are set on a pedestal of righteousness, but rather that the church recognizes these brothers and sisters as disciples who are striving to give their best to the service of their Lord and are living out their Christianity from that commitment.

At least one denomination sees as an extension of this exemplary role a ministry of reconciliation to be a vital part of the deacons' impact on the congregation. "If our congregations are indeed to be churches, we must learn to love our brothers and sisters *in spite of* their failings. A deacon can serve dual roles as a mediator and as a behavior model. The deacon's life can be a glowing example of creative Christian reconciliation" (197th Church of the Brethren Annual Conference Minutes, Baltimore, Maryland, 1983).

Witnesses. From what has been said above, it would follow that the life and testimony (written or oral) of the deacon will reflect the nature and commission of the church. The deacons, then, become very effective and essential agents for sharing with the total parish community the important events and opportunities in the congregation's worship and fellowship. The deacons can be the most effective group in the church to encourage renewal of faith and participation of those who are separated or inactive members. By keeping in touch regularly with those assigned to their shepherding group, deacons can personalize information about the church that will be of particular interest or help to individual families or persons; deacons can thus represent a contemporary version of the former annual deacons' visit which challenged people to evaluate their commitment and discipleship for Christ.

In turn the congregation has an obligation to give its deacons full respect and recognition for their set-apart calling. When new deacons are called, careful planning should be given to the commissioning service so that it reflects the significance of the office and clearly defines the ministry of deacons. Provision for training deacons for their servant roles, as well as provision for ongoing support for their responsibilities, must be made. Likewise, deacons should be acknowledged and thanked for significant services or programs for the congregation. Such recognition can be given through newsletter articles, pastors' reports, sermons, and other such means.

Every effort should be made to encourage members of the congregation to contact their deacon shepherd, or any other deacon with whom they feel comfortable, whenever they have a personal need or concern. Some congregations designate "deacons-of-the-month," persons who may be called for pastoral care in the event the pastor is away or cannot be reached. The program is periodically defined in the church newsletter to keep its purpose and helpfulness visible.

The effectiveness of deacons in the congregation is directly related to the significance of the ministry assigned to them and the affirmation they receive in fulfilling that ministry.

Deacons: An Integral Part of Pastoral Ministry

Jonathan C. Hunter

A positive and affirming relationship between the pastor and deacons is one of the most important elements in revitalizing the ministry of deacons within the congregation. As the pastor recognizes the deacons as an integral part of the "pastoral" ministry and willingly shares pastoral responsibility with them, the congregation will come to accept the work of deacons as a central part of the ministry of the church. As the pastor affirms the deacons in their work, the deacons will come to see the importance of their role in the congregation and will strive to be responsible to their calling.

The pastor plays an important role in developing a team relationship among the deacons. This is best done in some type of regular sharing/ training session. Though the pastor need not lead these sessions, it is critical that the pastor be present. When the pastor makes meetings of the deacons a priority, then the deacons will understand their importance to the pastor and to the congregation.

It may be that the pastor is the person best equipped to train deacons in the skills which are central to their task. However, in many congregations there are persons with extensive training in active listening and caring. For instance, a nurse who has a reputation as a sensitive and warm caregiver may be an excellent trainer for hospital visitation. Though other persons may do much of the concrete training, the pastor's presence is still critical. When the deacons see the pastor learning from skilled persons in the congregation, they will be more inclined to seek that help for themselves. The pastor is there to model for the deacons what it means to be open to refining and strengthening one's skills in the care of God's children. The pastor is also present to offer encouragement.

When I meet with the deacons in our congregation I make sure to speak directly about the importance of their work in the congregation. While being careful to preserve confidentiality, I share stories about the impact of the deacons' work on the life of the congregation. I share the gratitude of a parishioner who received a hospital visit from her deacons. I mention the couple who came to the Love Feast for the first time in five years after receiving a home visit from their deacons. These stories communicate my respect for their work and the regard I have for their calling.

Of course, not all of the experiences of deacons are positive. Then the pastor's role is to be an active listener and caregiver for the deacons. Over the past decades, clergy have discovered the value of sharing/support groups. Groups of clergy meet regularly to share with each other the joys and struggles of ministry. Within peer groups clergy find new resources for faithful ministry. The same need is felt by all who are in caregiving roles. We need a group of peers to listen to the hard stories. The pastor is present to model appropriate caring within the deacons' fellowship. The pastor is not there to rush into advice giving or problem solving. The first response is to listen attentively to what is said. Next, the pastor offers encouragement and support. Then, the pastor may lead the deacons in suggesting alternatives to help one another.

The deacons' fellowship thus becomes a model for the relationship of deacons to members of the congregation. The pastor and deacons are present to each other to listen and care. They are not there to solve each other's problems, but to help each one search for their own solutions.

This concept of modeling is central to the relationship between pastor and deacons and the relationship between deacons and persons in the congregation. What do we want the nature of that relationship to be? We want it to be defined by mutual respect, active listening on the part of the caregiver, a desire for each one to bear his or her own problems in so far as possible, and a high regard for the need for confidentiality in building trust relationships. How is the deacon to learn what such a relationship is like? We learn best by being in such a relationship ourselves.

The pastor, then, must strive to see that his or her relationship to each deacon is marked by those elements we have defined. Thus, the pastor does not relate to the deacon as an "expert" who is ready to pass on certain amounts of expertise to a consumer. Rather, the pastor relates to the deacon as a person of worth who has skills for caregiving. The pastor strives to respect the training, unique skills, and life experience of each deacon. The pastor actively listens to the stories told by the deacon. The pastor asks the deacon for help in understanding the story which is told and checks his or her understanding with the deacon. The pastor is careful not to take over the problems and successes of the deacon. The deacon is not bringing a broken item for the pastor to repair. The pastor tries to be as clear as possible about the ownership of any problems. The pastor then offers his or her own experience so that the deacon might discover new approaches to solving a current problem.

Confidentiality is both one of the most important aspects of this relationship and one of the most difficult to maintain. For me to share deeply of myself with another person I must have confidence that I am speaking only with that person, not with an entire congregation. To preserve confidentiality, I must never share what another has told me unless it is clear to me that the message was given to me to pass along. When it is difficult to determine whether I can share what has been said, I should ask permission: "Is this a concern which you would like to share with the other deacons?" By modeling this attitude with the deacons, the pastor makes it clear that they are not the "eyes and ears" of the pastor. Deacons should only share specific concerns with the pastor when they have asked permission: "Is this something you would like to share with the pastor? Might I share this concern with the pastor so that it might be kept in prayer?" The deacon should encourage the person to make his or her own appointment with the pastor. It is always second best for the deacon to ask the pastor to visit.

The sharing/training times for the deacons' fellowship provide another opportunity for modeling the relationship sought between deacons and persons in the congregation. As the pastor relates to this group of deacons, what each deacon has learned from his or her own relationship with the pastor is strengthened. Confidentiality is especially important in this setting. Rather than saying, "The Whites are having trouble with their marriage," the pastor might say, "I am having a hard time working with a couple on their marriage. I would appreciate you holding this concern in your prayers." (The pastor might have asked the Whites for permission to share the concern with particular deacons. In this case, the pastor might tell just those deacons that the Whites could use some extra understanding and support as they go through a difficult time in their relationship.) Likewise, when deacons share with each other in their support/training times, they are encouraged not to share the content of specific visits or encounters. Rather, they are encouraged to share about their own feelings as they deal with situations which are troubling or joyful.

The pastor and deacons thus become a source of spiritual strength and renewal for the entire congregation. They learn new skills for caring with each other and then live out those relationships with the larger body of Christ.

The Annual Deacon Visit: A Form of Pastoral Care

Karen Peterson Miller

Deeply instilled in the Anabaptist tradition is the careful attention given to spiritual development and to living peaceably with one's sister or brother. The relationships within a faith community are sustained in significant ways through a commitment to the beliefs and practices of the Anabaptist tradition. It is out of this understanding of nurturing spiritual development and living peaceably with all persons that the review of the Annual Visit is being considered as a form of pastoral care.

The biblical story as experienced in the nation of Israel, the ministry of Jesus, and the early Christian church tell us that nurturing the faith community was important. In the life of Israel the priests were the ones who stood before God as servants. They were considered to be agents of reconciliation and healing. Priests circulated in the community seeking to provide for the physical, relational, and spiritual needs. Jesus and his disciples visited throughout the countryside ministering to the spiritual, physical, and relational disorders of the community. Likewise in the early Christian churches, Paul and his helpers worked diligently to be sensitive and caring for those growing in their faith development. Paul and his followers made visiting the faith community for purposes of nurture a priority in their ministry.

At the Church of the Brethren Annual Meeting of 1867, a report about the purposes and activities of the visiting brethren was recorded. According to the minutes of the meeting, these brethren were an active and informed group who cared for the spiritual, physical, and relational aspects of congregational life. Once a year the visiting brethren would engage in a purposeful and meaningful discussion with each family concerning faith development.

"Annual Visit" as it came to be called was scheduled each year prior to the Love Feast gathering. This yearly visit was important and significant not only for the family but also for the well-being of congregational life. At the time of the visit it was the responsibility of the visiting brethren to ask the following questions:

1. Are you still in the faith as you were when you came into the church through baptism?
2. Are you at peace with your brothers and sisters, as far as you know?

3. Are you willing to work for more holiness in your life and in the lives of others?

4. Have you any matters to be brought before the church council? These questions concerned one's relationship with God and Jesus Christ as well as one's relationship within the community of believers. The visiting brethren were held accountable for reporting to the church council the well-being of all families visited.

The visiting brethren or deacons as they came to be called were required to answer the same questions for themselves as was indicated in the Annual Meeting minutes of 1889. They were to visit one another asking of each other the same questions. If everyone in the faith community had affirmed their relationship to God and their brothers and sisters, then the Love Feast could be celebrated.

In the process of reviewing the Annual Visit, it is significant to note that the questions covered vital aspects of beliefs and practices that are central to the Anabaptist tradition. Basic beliefs and practices that were addressed concerned baptism, peace and reconciliation, love and service. An exciting, invigorating discussion could develop focused around the heart of an individual faith experience as well as the heart of the corporate faith experience. The very questions themselves focused on the well-being (health, wholeness) of the whole body: spiritual, physical, emotional, and relational. Integration of the individual faith pilgrimage and the spiritual development of the congregation was a priority. Vitality of the fellowship in all phases of its development was nurtured.

During the 19th and early 20th century the Annual Visit by the deacons was an integral part of congregational life. However, when the professional ministry started to grow a decline occurred in the yearly use of the deacons as visitors. Deacons became the maintenance personnel for the congregation. Some of their custodial responsibilities included the preparation and serving of communion and the Love Feast, the visitation of the sick and bereaved, and the organizing of church suppers or special events. The ministry of nurture moved from being a responsibility of the deacons to the professional minister who was called to shepherd all persons. As a result of the decline in the nurturing aspects of the deacon program, the calling forth of deacons from the congregation to shepherd persons in their faith development became less intentional.

In reviewing the need for deacons in the Anabaptist tradition, it also seems appropriate to consider the need for revitalizing the Annual Visit. Since "the priesthood of all believers" is central to the tradition, as are baptism, reconciliation, and service, the calling of deacons and the renewing of their annual visits seems as appropriate for today as in earlier times. With the very real need for awareness, sensitivity, and caring love in our day, the church may have a special calling and responsibility. Revitalizing the deacons' visit, where persons minister to and with each other, can be a significant way of responding to that call.

Perhaps, the questions asked in the visit could be reformulated using the following wording:

1. Are you growing in the Christian faith?
2. As far as you are able to discern, are you at peace with your sisters and brothers?
3. How might you become a better steward of your talents and resources so that Christ may live more fully in you and others?
4. How might the congregation be more helpful to you in becoming a better steward of your spiritual gifts?

The questions provide persons an opportunity to review their life and faith journey as they move from the past, through the present, to the future. In addition to reviewing one's individual faith pilgrimage, a consideration of congregational growth and relationship is also provided. The questions allow persons to reaffirm their commitment to God, to the church, and to the world. Thus the intention of all who participate in the Annual Visit is that wholeness of life be nurtured and that all persons receive Christlike love.

Deacon Hospitality: A Holy Calling

Donald E. Miller

Deacons in the early church were given the task of caring for the tables, visiting the orphans and widows, and generally providing support ministries in the church. The tradition has split as to whether the deacons assist with the carrying out of worship. The caring for the tables and attending those who have special needs stand within the long biblical tradition of hospitality.

The book of Genesis already sharply divides those who hospitably receive the visitor and the stranger from those who abuse them. The three strangers who come to Abraham (Gen. 18) are graciously received, their feet washed, and a meal provided. When these same strangers go to Sodom, they are threatened by the Sodomites, who would wretchedly abuse them. The tone is set for a theme that runs throughout the Bible. God's people are those who receive and care not only for one another, but also for the needy and the stranger.

The hospitality theme becomes so prominent that pure religion is sometimes defined by caring for the widow, the orphan, and the stranger in your midst. (See Deut. 10:19; I Kings 17:8 ff.) As often as not, such care focuses in a meal. Israel comes to look forward to the time when people from all nations of the earth will be joined together in a hospitality meal. (See Isa. 25:6-8; Psa. 23:5.)

The New Testament continues the same theme, with hospitality regularly mentioned as one of the virtues of a Christian, along with humility, patience, and generosity. Jesus came eating and drinking, healing and caring for needy people, in contrast to John the Baptist who came fasting and generally staying removed from others. So it is not surprising that the early church wanted not only a worshiping, preaching community, but also an eating, drinking, healing, caring community. These various traditions of *diakonia* are part of the long theme of hospitality that is to be found throughout the Scriptures. In the New Testament the theme of hospitality is radicalized to the point that the stranger who is an enemy is also to be welcomed. That thought must have been as scandalous at the time as it is today, but it does show the seriousness and extent of the hospitality taught by the Scriptures.

The long history of the church has regularly featured the hospitality theme. Monastic orders often had a ritual of hospitality wherein the stranger was welcomed, the feet were washed, a meal was given, bedding was provided, and the stranger was sent on his or her way with a blessing of peace. The mark of hospitality has long been associated with Christian care.

The Lord's Supper was sometimes in the tradition of a hospitality meal. That is evident especially in the Gospel of Luke where the meal anticipates the final messianic banquet. The feeding of the five thousand in the Gospel of John was both a hospitality meal and a eucharistic celebration. The two meanings have split in the Christian tradition, so that the Lord's Supper is often a Passover meal for the faithful few. But for some the Lord's Supper is a hospitality meal, and the washing of feet is a link with an ancient tradition of welcoming all who come.

There are many ways in which the twentieth-century church can let *diakonia* be hospitality. The deacons can help the church take on the characteristics of welcoming the stranger and caring for those with special needs. Commonly, strangers are welcomed to a congregation by shaking their hands and having them stand up to be introduced in the service. Perhaps they are given a name tag or asked to sign the guest register.

The biblical accounts of welcoming the stranger go much farther than a friendly greeting. They move toward fellowship and a meal together wherein there is a genuine meeting of persons by an exchange of conversation about things that matter to one another. To the objection that such practices were appropriate in an ancient rural culture but not in a modern urban culture, the answer comes that twentieth-century urban people are in as much need of genuine communion with one another as people ever were.

Deacons might very well organize themselves or the whole congregation to offer an invitation to every church visitor, especially the stranger. These visitors can be invited to a home or a restaurant, but in either case provided with an opportunity for genuine fellowship. To have the congregation always prepared to offer such invitations will require training and organization. Perhaps every person or family unit in the congregation can offer to invite in a stranger once or several times a year. The deacons can keep a hospitality list, providing reminders and encouragement.

A related approach is to have one or more hospitality groups in the church. These groups make it a special concern to invite others to take part in their group. Such groups may range from Bible study to special activities like knitting or bowling. In any case, they are a means of inviting the stranger to take part. When people have participated in a hospitality group, they can be assisted to find other appropriate ways of relating to the church.

Once the deacons see themselves as a center of hospitality, only the imagination limits the group from finding ways to help the stranger feel welcome and included. The relationships may vary from a men's breakfast to a pork roast for the community, from an evening for the elderly to a prayer meeting. The point is to have groups searching for events to which strangers feel welcome.

Hospitality does not feature numbers so much as the communion, the fellowship, and the conversation. Nothing comes closer than making people feel physically comfortable (feetwashing) and participating in a meal together. If hospitality is extended with the Lord Jesus Christ in mind, then indeed the Lord will be present in the gathering.

Such activities as sponsoring refugees, visiting the sick, caring for the needy, and comforting the distressed are also unique expressions of hositality. In these acts, service to others and evangelism are combined in the theme of hospitality.

The suggestions about hospitality offered above are quite broad. Yet the central thrust is that of welcoming the stranger in an appropriate way, usually involving a fellowship meal together. So the deacon's task of waiting on tables is greatly extended in the biblical sense of hospitality. Being a deacon is more than an occasional ritual act. It is the call to help the whole congregation express the sense of hospitality that is found in the Scriptures. That is a holy calling and very much a part of the ministry of the church.

Deacons: Channels of God's Healing Spirit

Joan George Deeter

What qualities best equip persons for a caregiving ministry as deacons? Certainly the suggestions in 1 Timothy 3:8-13 merit our attention. We want deacons who are known for the sincerity of their commitment and the integrity of their lives. An authentic faith, devotion to the church, and a life-style respected by others in the faith community are important. Each congregation will be able to identify persons who represent the values they believe are essential.

Since primary attention is given here to the role of deacons in caring ministry, relational skills become priorities. We need deacons who know how to listen, who are comfortable enough with themselves to focus attention on the needs of the other, who are able to express love by either support or confrontation, who can be trusted to maintain confidentiality. We will also seek those who are gifted with the ability to communicate God's healing spirit.

And yet, before we assume we must find people whose journeys of faith have always been smooth and whose personal lives have proceeded without incident we should consider words from the book of Hebrews. In speaking of the priests appointed to relate to God on behalf of the people, the writer says: "He can deal gently with the ignorant and wayward, since he himself is beset with weakness. Because of this he is bound to offer sacrifice for his own sins as well as for those of the people" (Heb. 5:2-3 RSV). It is not the absence of turmoil that provides the best qualification for ministry; instead, equipping comes as faith is refined in the hot fire of personal agony. Those best able to sympathize with the weakness of others are those who have walked in similar paths.

The book of Joel provides a beautiful image for the strength that is formed from disappointment, despair, even destruction. Locusts have completely destroyed the land. Then comes a time of restoration. This is the framework in which the pouring out of the spirit on all flesh is promised (Joel 2:21-29 RSV). Joel provides a vivid description of total destruction followed by the assurance that . . . "it shall come to pass afterward, that I will pour out my spirit on all flesh; your sons and your daughters shall prophesy, your old men shall dream dreams, and your young men shall see visions. Even upon the menservants and maidservants in those days, I will pour out my spirit" (Joel 2:28-29 RSV).

There is the bare ground, the total destruction of the locusts, followed by restoration and the equipment for ministry. Roy Oswald focused on this image in a symposium on ministry; he gave credit to Carlyle Marney who explored this image in his book, *Beggars in Velvet*. Oswald suggests that there are some years in which it seems everything has been taken away. All those capable of breaking your heart have done just that. And it all comes up empty. This is an appropriate parallel to the totality of damage the locusts bring when they descend on crops. These six to seven inch insects destroy every leaf and blade in the years they come; and then the people drive their cattle over them to crush the locusts before they can lay their eggs and reproduce.

But that is not the end of the story in Joel, in our lives, or even in the areas of locust visitation. There is something special about those locust-laden fields. In the year following the visitation of the locusts, the fields now fertilized with the corpses of the locusts produce more than in any other year. And so it is with us; it is precisely our deepest hurts that provide the most solid base for ministry to one another in community.

Paul recognized this truth when he spoke of our carrying the treasure of God in earthen vessels to show forth the transcendent power that belongs to God and not to us. Death is at work in us, but also life (2 Cor. 4:7-12 RSV). And it is precisely this truth that equips us to extend ministry to others. Those who feel overwhelmed at times by the power of death are desperately in need of the assurance of the presence of life. And yet that assurance is more believable when it comes from one we know has walked the path of death, has survived the visitation of locusts.

Henri Nouwen, in his beautiful book, *The Wounded Healer*, calls it a great illusion of leadership to think we can be led out of a desert by someone who has never been there. Community is created, Nouwen feels, on the shared confession of our basic brokenness and our shared hope. That does not mean it is necessary to have spent time in the same desert as the person being served. It is, however, essential that the deacon know the reality of deserts.

Two stories provide reminders that bridges are built through shared pain. A couple had the opportunity to host friends with whom the only recent contact had been Christmas letters and a few brief, casual encounters. As they anticipated the visit, the host couple realized that the Christmas letters their friends had sent had created a kind of distance. The image presented in the letters was of the perfect family in which all the children had smoothly moved through the difficult passage of youth without significant problems. For the hosts, things had not moved that perfectly and the coming visit from their friends aroused guilt and anxiety.

What actually happened was that in the longer, more relaxed setting, more complete sharing took place. There was relief for the hosts in discovering that things had not been perfect for the visitors either. As pain was shared a new closeness resulted, as well as a commitment to hold one another's family in specific, intentional prayer.

The second story comes from a deeply committed Christian woman's journey through the devastation of substance abuse into wholeness and new life. This woman talks about the pain of years in which, although active in the church, she felt isolated from that community. She felt she must struggle alone with a problem too shameful to share with those who appeared to "have it all together." Even today she finds her best support in a group of others who have come through a similar experience and who speak honestly of their own problems and are willing to be openly confrontive with one another.

"A Christian community is therefore a healing community," Nouwen believes, " . . . because wounds and pains become openings or occasions for a new vision. Mutual confession then becomes a mutual deepening of hope, and sharing weakness becomes a reminder to one and all of the strength."

I believe this can be part of the deacon ministry, a more significant, meaningful community based on an increase in settings that encourage and enable persons to share the pain and struggle they often hide behind closed doors. Those best qualified to serve as deacons will be those who have themselves known brokenness, who have grown strong at the broken places, who have known God's strength most powerfully because of their own weakness, and who are willing to risk sharing their stories.

We have all known the devastation of locusts. And we have known the strength that comes as God leads us through those valleys. Our equipping as deacons comes from that sure interior knowledge and the courage to share. Those who are still in the midst of devastation may not be ready. We must be cautious in calling those who are still deformed by the wounds, who are stuck in bitterness, or who carry the kind of open sores for which there is a continuing need to seek attention and help.

Those most ready to serve as deacons are those who have experienced the joy of rebirth. Their lives are not perfect, but having received God's grace and power, they have the strength to reach out in healing to brothers and sisters who are at various points along that same path. Deacons thus qualified will bless us all.

The Caregiving Functions of Deacons

Anita Smith Buckwalter

Numerous functions of ministry are apparent in the New Testament. This resource will address seven important functions for deacons in the church in our day. Readers will recognize from Harold Bauman's article, "Variations in Anabaptist Traditions," that several of these functions have been carried out by deacons during the history of the Believers Church. These caregiving functions are: (1) serving, (2) nurturing, (3) healing, (4) worshipping, (5) discipling, (6) advocating, and (7) presence.

It is our purpose, in so categorizing the functions of deacons, to provide to congregations some handles for assigning roles and providing resources for deacons.

These caregiving functions of deacons are based on the following assumptions:

1. There is a deacon *body* within the congregation. It is not expected that any individual person be qualified or have the gifts to become qualified to serve all of these functions. It is expected that within the deacon body many of the needed gifts will be found (1 Cor. 12:4-11; Rom. 12:4-8).
2. Congregations will choose deacons who are spiritually mature, sensitive to the needs of individuals and the congregation, open to the moving of the Holy Spirit, and willing to learn new skills and new ways of functioning.
3. The deacon body works in close consultation and cooperation with the pastor(s) and other chosen leaders in the congregation. The apostle Paul encourages us to have the mind and attitude of Christ among us as we show kindness and compassion to one another (Phil. 2:2-5).
4. By expanding and enhancing the ministry of deacons, we can begin to reclaim some of our Believers Church heritage of "the priesthood of all believers."

Serving

The most common function of deacons in our congregations is that of serving. The name "deacon" comes from the Greek word for servant, *diakonos*. This serving function is illustrated in Acts 6:1-8 where additional leaders were needed in the fellowship to oversee the daily distribution of food to the widows.

In our time deacons serve as they meet the physical and material needs of members of the congregation, or the congregation as a whole. Many congregations have a contingency fund to provide for emergency material aid, such as food, clothing, and shelter. In some groups this is actually called the "Deacons' Fund" and is administered by the deacon board. In one congregation this fund has been used for a variety of needs: to pay a security deposit on a new apartment for a battered woman and her three children, to pay utilities for the family of a disabled man who was caught in the time lag between disability payments and insurance reimbursements, and as a loan to a family with an unexpected tax bill.

Deacons establish various types of financial systems within the congregation to ensure that material needs are met. In some congregations the deacons administer student loan funds for post-high school education and training. In others they initiate and operate campership funds so that all the children of the congregation and some from the community can attend summer church camp regardless of family income.

One particular aspect of the serving function is hospitality. Deacons may arrange for members of the congregation to provide meals, transportation, or child care for families where there is a new baby, prolonged illness, or death. Similar material aid may be needed by recently arrived refugees, or families who have sent one of their members for extended ministries such as disaster rebuilding, disaster child care, or counseling at church camp. The hospitality function of the deacon board may extend to being responsible for welcoming persons who visit the congregation's Sunday worship services.

Deacons serve the physical needs of the congregation as a whole by attending to the physical preparations needed for Love Feast and baptism. Deacons are servants as they enhance a congregation's offerings of hospitality and material aid following Paul's counsel: "Share with God's people who are in need. Practice hospitality" (Rom. 12:13 NIV).

Nurturing

Deacons fulfill a nurturing function as they meet the spiritual and emotional needs of church members; this contrasts with the serving function which meets physical and material needs. These tasks of spiritual and emotional nurturing are sometimes labeled "pastoral care" or "shepherding." Some congregations call such ministry "undershepherding" to distinguish it from the pastoral care provided by the clergy of the congregation.

Deacons provide nurture as they organize and implement prayer chains in congregations. Deacon caregivers call, visit, and pray with persons who are experiencing hard times such as unemployment, bereavement, parent-child tension, and spiritual barrenness. Such deacon nurturing follows the apostle Paul's counsel to "carry one another's burdens and so fulfill the law of Christ" (Gal. 6:2), and to "rejoice with those who rejoice; mourn with those who mourn" (Rom. 12:15). Deacons may develop and maintain a program of small shepherding groups in the church family, perhaps even serving as leaders for each group. Such groups provide the vital contact with families and individuals in the congregation necessary to discover needs and provide appropriate support. They are also important avenues for assisting spiritual development and growth in Christian discipleship.

Deacons may also be called to take special responsibility for visiting shut-ins and remembering them at special times, caroling at Christmas, delivering flowers at Easter, and initiating card showers on birthdays. Deacons often care for ill and hospitalized church members by sending cards and gifts in the name of the church family and supplementing the visits of the pastor.

The nurturing deacon walks beside Christian sisters and brothers, giving encouragement, bringing comfort and help in the same way that God in Christ has encouraged, comforted, and helped them (2 Cor. 1:3-4).

Healing

Deacons are called to initiate and participate in the healing ministries of the congregation, physical, emotional, relational, and spiritual healing. Deacons may function as the elders who are called to pray for those who are ill (Jas. 5:14-16). Deacons can actively invite persons to consider anointing, and then in consultation with the pastor make arrangements for the anointing and assist with the service.

In some congregations several deacons accompany the pastor on visits with couples having marital difficulties or families in crisis; they provide additional encouragement and help to find possibilities for reconciliation. In other congregations the deacon body takes responsiblity for ministry to inactive members, which often involves relational and spiritual healing.

The deacon body may function as the congregation's mediation group, facilitating the process described in Matthew 18:15-20 in conflicts between individuals or groups within the congregation. As non-partisan facilitators, the deacons can help to bring about reconciliation and redemption in the conflict situation, preserve the integrity of the church, encourage Christian conduct and attitudes, and nurture loyalty to Christ and the church.

Deacons function as healers as they live and move among their Christian sisters and brothers, meeting them in their hurts and enabling them to experience wholeness.

Discipling

The discipling function of deacons includes both helping members in the church evaluate the authenticity of their faith and calling disciples in the church to a deeper commitment. The discipling function places the task of cultivating responsible membership in the congregation with the deacon body.

Deacons can be helpful in challenging the members of the church, through regular communication and sensitive encouragement, to be faithful to their baptismal vows. In some congregations the deacons have responsibility for cultivating prospective members and inviting them to consider membership. Often deacons act as "sponsors" of new members and provide personal nurture following their baptism or reception into the church.

Deacons may be given responsibilty for periodically reviewing the membership list of the church and recommending to the church board or council the classification for those who have not participated in the life and ministry of the congregation for a specified period of time.

In some congregations deacons function as the nominating committee for the various offices of the church, discerning gifts and calling members to serve. They may organize a talent bank for sharing human and material resources of the congregation as needed.

In discipling, deacons "speak the truth in a spirit of love" to assist persons in growing up in every way to Christ. Discipling helps each separate part of the Body work as it should so that the whole Body grows and builds itself up through love (Eph. 4:11-16).

Worshipping

Deacons in the Anabaptist tradition a few generations ago functioned much more as worship leaders than they do today. For example, deacons often led the congregational singing and prayers. Currently deacon involvement in worship leadership is primarily confined to planning and assisting with the observance of communion and the Love Feast, although in some congregations deacons provide worship leadership and preach when the pastor is absent.

Deacon bodies who carry responsiblity for the overall spiritual health of the congregation may find ways to consult with and advise the pastor(s) about the congregation's corporate worship life and may assist periodically in worship leadership. The deacons might appoint a representative to the worship committee, or establish such a committee if the congregation does not have one. Deacons might also find ways to encourage personal devotional life and family worship experiences.

Worshipping is an important dimension within many of the other functions of deacon caregiving. Prayer, reading scripture, and sharing faith experiences can be vital aspects of serving, nurturing, healing, discipling, advocating, and the ministry of presence. "Let the word of Christ dwell in you richly as you teach and admonish one another with all wisdom, and as you sing psalms, hymns and spiritual songs with gratitude in your hearts to God" (Col. 3:16). Persons in need often are looking for the unique and special quality that worship adds to the care they receive.

In small group or "one-to-one" worship experiences it is important that the deacon caregiver be sensitive so that the style and timing of prayer and scripture reading are appropriate to the situation and the persons involved. It is inappropriate to use prayer as a way to manipulate others or as a technique for ending visits. Prayer is most effective as the act of sharing the needs of the moment with God and requesting God's wisdom and power for those needs. The content of worship should always be relevant to the needs of persons receiving care. 2 Timothy 3:16 identifies the giving of instruction and the correcting of errors as uses of scripture; depending on a person's needs, sharing scripture can also provide comfort and hope.

Worshipping can be an important reminder for both the caregiver and care-receiver of the power available for all our needs—the creative and sustaining power of God, the healing and freeing power of Christ, the comforting and strengthening power of the Holy Spirit.

Advocating

Advocates are persons who plead another's cause. Advocates also are persons who speak or write in support of some cause or idea. Deacons are called to both types of advocacy ministry.

Deacons need to be advocates for individuals or groups in the congregation who have no voice in decision making, or those whose voices are not listened to, or whose needs are not being met. Such persons or groups vary from one congregation to another. They may be the children or the senior citizens, single persons or young adults, disabled persons or those who speak another language. Jesus was an advocate for the voiceless of his day. He defended the prostitute who came into the home of Simon the Pharisee to anoint him (Luke 7:36-50). And he rebuked his impatient disciples by saying, "Let the little children come to me, and do not hinder them . . . " (Mark 10:13-16). Congregations may not be able to provide facilities and services for all the special needs of individuals; but the deacon body can be the group who weighs the needs and the resources to find some resolution to the situation.

Deacons are called also to be advocates for the values and programs of the congregation and the wider church family. Paul's letter to Titus describes the "elder" (or deacon) as one who "must hold firmly to the trustworthy message as it has been taught, so that he can encourage others by sound doctrine and refute those who oppose it" (Tit. 1:9 NIV). Deacons are advocates as they interpret the teachings and practices of the church in classes, small groups, and the community: "We stand for *these* values." "These things are important to us."

Presence

The ministry of presence is a gift of the Holy Spirit who reveals God's activity to people through the life, the being, the presence of the one ministering. When our lives embody the gospel in such a way that others notice and are led to the truth, then we are involved in the caring ministry of presence. (See 1 John 4:12-17.)

The ministry of presence may seem like a new idea to some in the Believers Church tradition. Often those of Germanic descent can identify more readily with doing good works. But presence is an important function of deacons, as the following story illustrates.

Bob and Russ became acquainted when Bob and his wife rented the upstairs apartment in Russ's home. Three years later when they were expecting their first child, Bob and his wife bought their own home. But Bob had developed such a high regard for Russ that the two stayed in touch with occasional letters and visits.

Fifteen years passed; one afternoon Russ experienced a strong urge to visit Bob. He discovered that Bob had been hurt in a fall and was home from work. During a long, tearful conversation Bob confessed that he had a drinking problem and was failing in relationship with his son. But he was reluctant to enter treatment for fear of a blot on his record. Russ left with a big hug and a promise to pray for Bob. Two days later Bob's wife called to tell Russ that they were leaving for a treatment center. Within a year Bob and his wife began attending church with Russ. Bob told Russ, "It was not what you said. It was not what you did. It is who you are and that you were there." It was the ministry of presence. Russ's presence represented Christ-conveyed consolation, encouragement, and strength when it was needed.

Deacons also serve in the ministry of presence as they are model lay people. 1 Timothy 3:8-13 calls deacons to lead exemplary lives which "gain a good standing for themselves." 1 Timothy 4:12 encourages, "Don't let anyone look down on you because you are young, but set an example for the believers in speech, in life, in love, in faith, and in purity" (NIV). Deacons are not set-apart in quite the same way as pastors, so deacons can be an example and witness to how strong Christian commitment and involvement can be mixed with employment in the "secular" world. At the same time, deacons *are* set-apart in the sense that they are named as leaders in the congregation and thus carry some authority and representation of the Body of Christ.

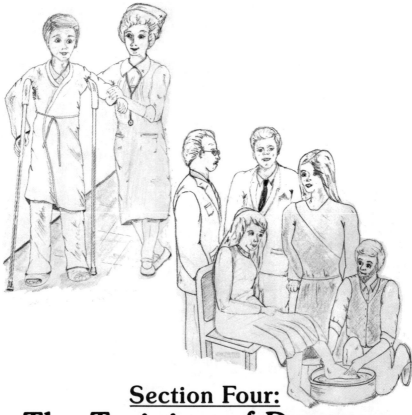

Section Four:
The Training of Deacons

Elements of a Deacon Training Program

James M. Lapp

Congregations need to train their members for ministry. No responsibility is more crucial to the long-term health and effective functioning of God's people than the time and energy invested in "the equipment of the saints for the work of ministry" (Eph. 4:11 RSV).

The word "equipment" in first century Greek referred to a physician setting a broken bone or putting a joint back into place. When congregational leaders give primary attention to enabling the ministry of all church members, the results are a healthy, well-coordinated body. When leaders jealously seek to control all activities of the church or fail to equip all members for ministry, the members spiritually wither and the life forces of the body are impeded.

In many congregations there are professionally trained persons who show high levels of competence in many aspects of ministry. Some will have gifts readily available for and oriented toward the service of deacon. Others will need (desire) special equipping to prepare them for the particular ministry of the diaconate.

There are six important elements for a comprehensive deacon training program. They are (1) personal growth, (2) modeling, (3) teaching/instruction, (4) apprenticing, (5) evaluation, and (6) support/renewal.

1. Personal Growth

When we consider the task of training for ministry, we often think first of skills to be learned and perfected. Certainly skills are important. But more important than highly polished technique or academic degrees is the degree of self-awareness and personal maturity possessed by a deacon. The ability to minister effectively to others will be in proportion to the attention deacons have given to their own growth.

Enabling people to be in touch with their own weaknesses and strengths, to experience liberation from guilt and self-defeating patterns of life, to enjoy a positive and accurate view of themselves, to understand their typical responses to criticism and conflict, to know how others perceive them interpersonally, are all important aspects of personal training essential to a useful ministry. Sermons, retreats, special classes, workshops, small caring groups, counseling, and spiritual direction are all settings in which this type of intentional growth can occur.

Often an area of presumed weakness will become one's greatest asset when a person is willing to embrace it. As Ernest Hemingway once wrote, " . . . life breaks us all and afterward many are strong at the broken places." The beauty of God's grace is never so brilliant as it is against the backdrop of our own earthiness (2 Cor. 4:7).

2. Modeling

Training for ministry does not begin at a certain age; nor is it limited to formal settings. It occurs throughout our lives through the modeling of persons we observe in the sum total of our experience in the church.

Theologically, modeling finds its basis in the incarnation of Jesus. God communicated with us, not through a manuscript, but through a living example. Jesus gathered twelve persons around him for the purpose of training them for leadership in God's kingdom. He recognized that effective training will result in disciples becoming like their teacher (Luke 6:40). Paul boldly invited those to whom he ministered to imitate him (1 Cor. 4:16; Phil. 3:17).

The potential for training through modeling can be greatly enhanced by planning deliberate settings where others can observe leaders in action. Inviting less experienced persons to go along while making visits in the hospital, nursing home, or family setting; letting them observe others as they exercise leadership in meetings or minister in times of crisis; or listening while a group of deacons discusses issues or concerns in their work—all of these may become helpful opportunities for training. While modeling makes one quite vulnerable, it also enables people to gain a realistic picture of the diaconate, and can allow even one's seeming failures to become occasions for another's growth.

3. Teaching/Instruction

Training will likely include formal occasions for instruction in various aspects of the deacon's ministry. Contemporary psychology has accumulated many valuable insights into such areas as techniques for communication, positive ways to deal with conflict, the unique needs of youth, the challenges of mid-life, the processes of aging, the emotional and spiritual needs of people who are hospitalized or seriously ill, the impact of the nuclear threat on children—all of which can be taught to caregivers.

Not to be overlooked in teaching are practical ways to use the Scriptures and prayer in ministry with those in need. Kenneth Haugk writes that "to ignore the traditional resources of Christianity in a caring situation would be much like a physician choosing not to use medical equipment during surgery" (*Christian Caregiving*). We dare not assume these resources for ministry are readily available in a deacon's repertoire of skills.

This teaching will likely occur in a variety of settings—sermons, Sunday school classes, workshops, retreats, and special training sessions. Creativity in teaching coupled with an aliveness of the Spirit and many practical illustrations from human experience will be essential ingredients in making this training a truly equipping experience for deacons.

4. Apprenticing

Apprenticing is essentially the training of the less experienced by the more experienced. In the mentor model for apprenticing, a beginner in ministry forms an intentional relationship with a more competent person to learn all he or she can by observation, discussion, and involvement under the direction of the "teacher." For centuries this was the primary method for teaching a trade. Missionary statesman D. T. Niles says that being a disciple is more like being an apprentice at a trade than a student in the classroom. Might one helpful pattern for equipping deacons be to develop an intentional relationship between a novice and an experienced leader for a designated period of time?

A second model of apprenticing, supervision, has long been used in the training of teachers, chaplains, and doctors. Could it also be used in the training of deacons? Supervision provides regular opportunities for conversation and feedback through which persons can learn from their successes and failures. A supportive supervisor can provide clarity of focus for one's ministry. The safety and security of knowing you are not alone in your initial attempts at ministry can do much to build confidence and turn an awesome challenge into a meaningful occasion of learning.

5. Evaluation

Evaluation is frequently a neglected aspect of training for ministry. It holds considerable potential for learning when it includes gentle accountability, helpful reflection, and constructive counsel on how one's service can be improved. Without evaluation we may either wallow in discouragement or become oblivious to well-rehearsed but ineffective patterns of ministry.

Harold Bauman, in *Congregations and Their Servant Leaders*, suggests that there are three questions a supervisor can ask of a person seeking to grow in ministry:
1. What went reasonably well in your ministry and why?
2. What did not go well and why?
3. How can improvement be made the next time in your ministry?

Persons could be invited annually to engage in a more thorough evaluation by writing a two or three page summary of their service during the past year, noting strengths and weaknesses and goals for growth in ministry. Many persons are too severe in evaluating themselves. For this reason we need the reflections of other persons. A trusted colleague, a person to whom one has ministered, and a supervisor could each write a review of the person's service. Under the careful guidance of a good supervisor, this process could result in constructive learning for a deacon.

6. Support/Renewal

For the ministry of deacons to be personally satisfying, helpful to others, and honoring to God, deacons need adequate structures for support and renewal. Deacons will evidence the usual symptoms of stress and burn out quickly if they neglect to establish and nurture supportive relationships. To be sure, the pastor may well provide one such relationship for a deacon. The deacons themselves can be a strong source of support to one another. But outside of these colleagues in ministry, deacons need persons who love and accept them without regard for their office in the church.

In addition to enjoying supportive relationships with other persons, deacons need to be assisted in developing a growing relationship with God. Paul's counsel to Timothy was to "train yourself in godliness" (1 Tim. 4:7 RSV). While physical fitness is necessary, it is no substitute for disciplining ourselves in the time-honored patterns of authentic spirituality.

Equipping the saints will include providing them with all the resources needed for their success in ministry. Warnings about the temptations common to deacons and practical instruction on how to maintain a vibrant relationship with God amidst the inordinate pressures of life are dimensions of training not to be ignored.

It should be noted further that training for deacon ministry is an ongoing process. Sharpening relational skills, evaluating results, receiving and giving support are lifelong processes by which we continue to grow. A congregation that is intentional in its deacon training program will provide a variety of opportunities on a continuing basis to challenge growth, no matter how experienced their deacons are.

The rewards of such training will be enjoyed by the whole congregation as people are enabled to enter more freely and confidently into their respective areas of service. The highest compliment will be the "well done" received from God by these faithful servants, both those doing the training and those being trained (Matt. 25:21).

Training Sessions for Equipping Deacons

Neta Jackson

DOING IT—HOW TO USE THIS TRAINING DESIGN

To the pastor or training leader:

The articles in this manual are a valuable resource for those who desire to restore or enhance the role of deacon in the congregation. As pastor, church board, or elders, you now have the task of channeling these resources through caregivers—those called to be deacons—to help meet the actual needs of persons in your congregation.

Stop! Before you go any further . . .

Before you get into the specifics of how to use this training design, read "Elements of a Deacon Training Program" by James Lapp, (p.79 of this resource). The six dimensions of training that he discusses are essential in equipping your deacons. While all six are used to a certain degree in the following training sessions, the very nature of "training sessions" relies heavily on the "teaching/instruction" dimension. "Personal growth" is an ongoing process in the life of each deacon which needs to be encouraged, as "modeling" is an ongoing dimension that you must recognize and provide. "Apprenticing" is on-the-job training, while "evaluation" and providing for "support and renewal" need to happen periodically.

To understand more fully your role in the training of deacons, read "Deacons: An Integral Part of Pastoral Ministry" by Jonathan C. Hunter (p. 55), and "The Caregiving Team" by Al Dueck (p.23), especially Section II "Lay/Formal Caregivers."

Now, on to the nitty gritty!

Who are these training sessions for?

These training sessions assume that you have already discerned those with gifts of caregiving and have appointed these deacons to serve. The sessions will not only give these deacons opportunity to learn about the functions of deacons and a chance to practice caregiving skills but will also become a means of giving care to the deacons themselves.

It is also possible to join together with one or more congregations in your area for these training sessions. While making the group size larger, you nonetheless benefit from a broader range of experience and support.

Who should lead these sessions?

The pastor, a member of the church board, one of the elders, or an experienced deacon—or, if possible, a team of at least two of the above persons—should fulfill this role. A primary function of the session leader(s) is to model both the skills and functions of caregiving; team leadership provides a broader base of experience to share with your deacons.

Be alert for ways to use additional resource persons in the training sessions: members of your congregation who are involved in professional caregiving (doctors, nurses, counselors, social workers, physical therapists); persons with particular experience and skills, such as family financial planning or early childhood development—anything that might help your deacons learn ways to minister to various needs.

Finally, expect that the training participants will not only be "learners" but also "teachers" and "support persons" for each other. Each will have gifts and experiences to share with the rest, and all of these become a vital part of the learning process.

What is the framework for the training sessions?

Basic training. A suggested time-frame is one session per week for six weeks. This has the advantage of concentrating on the training for a fairly short period of time, giving your deacons some basic knowledge and skills, and getting them launched.

Extended training. You may want to lengthen your training program to one session every four weeks over a period of six months. This has the advantage of allowing more on-the-job training between sessions (e.g., doing visitation with the pastor or an experienced deacon); the disadvantage is delaying some necessary skill training and understanding of deacon functions until later in the process.

Weekend retreat. One more possible structure is a weekend retreat. This has the advantage of developing a high degree of fellowship and support among the deacons, as they come apart for three days together, away from other distractions and responsibilities. It also gives the deacons an overview of the various functions and basic skills early in the process. The challenge, of course, is concentrating six training sessions into one weekend! This framework gives very little time for personal reflection between sessions, nor does it allow for actual caregiving situations as part of the training process. However, these could be part of an ongoing process after the retreat.

A retreat schedule might look like this:

Friday evening:	(8-10 p.m.)	Session I
Saturday morning:	(8-10 a.m.)	Session II
	(10:30-12:30)	Session III
Saturday afternoon:	(4-6 p.m.)	Session IV
Saturday evening:	(8-10 p.m.)	Session V
Sunday morning:	(9-10 a.m.)	Worship
	(10-12 a.m.)	Session VI
Sunday afternoon:	(1:30-3:30)	Planning for Implementation

Ongoing Deacon Support Structure. Whatever training design you use, a process of evaluation, support, and additional training is imperative. The last session provides a framework for ongoing training to help deacons understand specific needs (divorced persons, the elderly, the grief process, bridging cultural barriers, farmers in crisis, international students, depending on the specific caregiving needs in your congregation), as well as a framework for evaluation and support.

How are the sessions structured?

Each session is planned for a two-hour time frame. Each session is built around one of the *caregiving functions* outlined in "The Caregiving Functions of Deacons" by Anita Smith Buckwalter (p. 71). Most sessions will also focus on a basic *caregiving skill* which relates to the function in focus; many of the skills, of course, are important in a variety of deacon functions.

A final word . . .

Jonathan Hunter says, "How is the deacon to learn what such a relationship (caregiving that involves mutual respect, active listening, trust, and confidentiality) is like? We learn best by being in such a relationship ourselves" (p. 56).

As training leader, your primary role is one of relationship. You and your deacons are present for each other to listen and to care. You are not there to give "expert answers" or to solve their problems for them, but to help each one search for their own solutions. You model the relationship that the deacons will carry to members of the congregation as they go forth to serve.

Preparation for the First Session:

- Buy a notebook to use as a journal during the training period. Your journal will also serve as a helpful way to reflect on your experiences in caregiving situations for continued growth and evaluation.

- Read the following articles in this manual:
  "A Call to Caring" by Lenora Stern (p. 15).
  "A Brief Biblical/Historical Perspective" by Erland Waltner (p. 29).
  "The Image and Ministry of Deacons Within the Congregation" by Fred W. Swartz (p. 51).
  "The Caregiving Functions of Deacons" by Anita Smith Buckwalter (p. 71).

- Meditate on the experience of Jesus and the disciples in John 13.

Session 1
What Is Christian Caring?

"Now that I, your Lord and Teacher, have washed your feet, you also should wash one another's feet. . . . Love one another. As I have loved you, so you must love one another" (John 13:14, 34 NIV).

Focusing Your Objective:

    To discover the biblical vision of love and service as the basis for the role of deacons in the church; to understand what is unique about *Christian* caregiving; and to explore serving persons with physical and material needs as a specific function of deacons in the church.

GETTING STARTED

- Indicate that the primary resources for these training sessions will come from materials in *Called to Caregiving: A Resource for Equipping Deacons in the Believers Church*, and from your own experiences as you share with the group. Learning how to support one another in a variety of caregiving situations is a prime objective of these sessions together.

- Divide the group into pairs, and ask persons to share the following:
    1. What was my concept of the role of deacon as a youth? As an adult?
    2. What caregiving experience(s) have I had as a deacon? As a professional caregiver? Other?

- If the group is small (eight persons or less), introduce your partner to the rest of the group, sharing briefly his or her responses to the questions above. (With a larger group, divide into small groups of four to six.)

THE VISION: DEACONS AS CAREGIVERS

Exploring the Biblical Basis:
- Read and discuss briefly this statement by Erland Waltner: "The central meaning of serving as a deacon comes directly from the teaching and pattern of Jesus. Jesus is the archetype of the deacon. Therefore, to function as a deacon, in the biblical perspective, is to serve, to minister, to help" (p.29).

- Read aloud the following New Testament scriptures in the group, and discuss the suggested questions:

  Mark 9:35; Mark 10:43-45; John 13:14
    1. What is the basic attitude Jesus addresses in these scriptures?

  Matthew 27:55; Matthew 25:35-36; Acts 9:36, 39
    1. What forms of practical service are mentioned here?
    2. Who are the recipients of this service?
    3. Who are the caregivers?

  Acts 6:2-4; Acts 19:22
    1. What role did these helpers play in the preaching of the gospel?
    2. In what other ways did Stephen, Philip, and Timothy minister in the early church?

  Ephesians 4:11-13; 1 Corinthians 12:4-6; 1 Peter 4:9-10
    1. What is the primary goal for the exercise of the various gifts and ministries mentioned in these verses?

  Philippians 1:1; 1 Timothy 3:8-12; Romans 16:1
    1. These scriptures refer not only to attitudes and acts of service, but to a role or office. What are the implications here in relation to other roles or offices in the church?
    2. What are the qualifications listed in 1 Timothy for deacons and "wives" (also "women," possibly "deaconesses")? Considering the role, why are these qualifications important?

What is *Christian* Caring?

- Share your responses to the following questions in the group:
    1. What is *Christian* about caring done by Christians?
    2. Are we trying to give care that is actually better done by professionals and social service agencies?
    3. With all the needs around us, are there some persons or groups to whom we have a particular responsibility?

- Consider the following: The apostle Paul exhorts the church in Rome to be "contributing to the *needs of the saints*, practicing hospitality" (Rom. 12:13). He also challenges the churches in Galatia, "So then, while we have opportunity, let us do good to all men, and especially to those who are of the household of the faith" (Gal. 6:10). Elsewhere in scripture we are called to give a "cup of cold water" in Jesus' name to any person in need. Yet Paul points to a particular responsibility to care for the needs of other believers. How do you understand these two points of view?

- Respond to Kenneth C. Haugk's view of Christian caring. In his book, *Christian Caregiving—A Way of Life*, Haugk says, "The term *body of Christ* describes people united by Jesus Christ into a real community. This 'family-ness' of Christianity entails both benefits and responsibilities . . . . Ultimately, the right to care flows from our responsibility as family members."[1]

    Still, there remains the question, "What is distinctively *Christian* caregiving?" In addressing this question, Haugk says: "Farmers teach lessons in hope every day. . . . As a farmer's responsibility rests with preparing a crop for harvest, so the Christian caregiver's responsibility is to 'plant' and 'water.' God then provides the growth. In other words, *Christians* are responsible for care; God is responsible for cure. . . . Like other caregivers, Christians work hard to establish relationships that build up people in need. Christian caregivers, however, rely on God for results. . . . You carry the news of his unconditional acceptance and hope-filled gospel of forgiveness and life in him. Caring is a process—like tilling, fertilizing, planting, and cultivating. Processes are verbs, and the process of caring is in your hands. Results are nouns, and cures (the results of your caring) are in God's hands."[2]

1. How does understanding God as the Curegiver free us to be caregivers?
2. What can we bring to caregiving that is distinctively Christian?
3. Recall in the article, "A Call to Caring," how Lenora Stern uses the biblical story of the paralyzed man let down through a roof by his friends as an example of caregiving. How does this story illustrate the relationship between our role as caregivers and God's role as Curegiver?

EXPLORING THE FUNCTIONS OF DEACONS: SERVING

- Review Anita Smith Buckwalter's overview of "The Caregiving Functions of Deacons" (p. 71). Then discuss in the group:
    1. Which of the seven functions mentioned have been operating in our congregation? Through whom? In what way?
    2. Which functions could be strengthened? Through whom and in what way?
    3. Are there any functions mentioned here that seem to apply to the role of deacon in our congregation more than others? Why?

- Read aloud Buckwalter's section, Serving (p. 71). Discuss:
    1. Although serving describes all gifts that minister to others and build up the body of Christ, how does Buckwalter specifically focus the serving function for deacons?
    2. In our congregation, what are some of the material and physical needs we might need to give attention to as deacons? (financial aid for unemployed, hospitality for international students, meals for new parents) Be specific.

GROUP RESPONSE

- Read and reflect on Lenora Stern's statement, "I suggest that we, as disciples, need to be *assertive servants* in caring for others in the family, in the congregation, and in the neighborhood. . . . The term assertive implies that one makes an intentional choice to act, to get involved. . . . Christians are to love every brother and sister whether or not the love is returned. In fact, as Christians, we are to extend love even to those whose lifestyle or behavior is undesirable, rather than confine our love only to those who mirror our own values" (pp. 15-16).

- Ask the group: "What barriers do you feel or experience which hinder you from taking the initiative to love and serve your brothers and sisters?" Record responses on a chalkboard or sheet of newsprint for all to see.

Assignment:
- Ask yourselves: Is there a physical or material need in our congregation that needs immediate attention this week? If so, what can we do? (If possible, team a new deacon with a more experienced deacon, pastor, or other church leader to respond to this need.)

- Identify possible barriers you fear or might experience in initiating love in this situation.

- Pray for each other, for God's help in overcoming these barriers to loving service.

YOUR PERSONAL JOURNEY

In Your Journal:
- Reread 1 Timothy 3:8-12. List the qualifications for deacons in your journal.

- Ask yourself: In which areas do I need most to grow? What barriers (fears, hindrances) do I personally experience in initiating loving service toward a person in need? Ask for God's help in overcoming these barriers.

Steps to Take:
- Is there a physical or material need among my own family members (or coworkers at work) that could be met if I took the initiative to serve? (Does my spouse need a night off for personal recreation, rest, or renewal? Is there a household chore or repair that isn't getting done? Is there an errand or "chauffeuring duty" I could do for one of my children or any other nondriver?) DO IT.

Preparation for the Next Session:
- Read the following articles in this manual:
  "Deacon Hospitality: A Holy Calling" by Donald E. Miller (p. 63).
  "The Caring Congregation" by Larry Martens (p. 19).
  "The Caregiving Team" by Al Dueck (p. 23).

- Meditate on 2 Corinthians 1:3-7.

Session 2
Discovering
Caring Opportunities

Praise be to the God and Father of our Lord Jesus Christ, the Father of compassion and the God of all comfort, who comforts us in all our troubles, so that we can comfort those in any trouble with the comfort we ourselves have received from God" (2 Cor. 1:3-4 NIV).

Focusing Your Objective:
To focus on caring for spiritual and emotional needs as a specific function of deacons; to understand how various changes in a person's life create opportunities for caring; and to explore hospitality as one specific avenue of caring.

GETTING STARTED

- Review your discussion at the close of the last session. Did you identify a physical or material need in the congregation that you would address? Review what happened. How was the need addressed? What was the response of the person(s) in need? What are the thoughts and feelings of those who served? Share with the group.

- Choose a partner and take turns sharing what happened with your personal challenge from the last session: Were you able to serve a family member or co-worker in a special way with a physical or material need? How did you feel serving in this way?

EXPLORING THE FUNCTIONS OF DEACONS: NURTURING

Nurturing Structures:
- Read aloud in the group Anita Smith Buckwalter's section, Nurturing (p. 72). Discuss:
  1. What distinction does Buckwalter make between serving and nurturing?
  2. Why is it important to understand the difference?

- Consider Buckwalter's statement, "Deacons may develop and maintain a program of small shepherding groups in the church family, perhaps even serving as leaders for each group. Such groups provide the vital contact with families and individuals in the congregation necessary to discover needs and provide appropriate support. They are also important avenues for assisting spiritual development and growth in Christian discipleship" (pp. 72-73).
    1. Why does Buckwalter suggest that the small group structure is a good way to nurture the spiritual and emotional needs of a congregation?
    2. If our congregation uses small groups, are they shepherding groups or task groups? Do the group leaders function as deacons?
    3. If our congregation were to develop shepherding groups, would we need more deacons than have been designated already?
    4. Which of our present congregational programs and structures nurture the emotional and spiritual needs of each member?
    5. What other "structures" might our congregation develop to care for the shepherding needs of the congregation?

Sources of Caring:

- Read aloud the following statements:

    Larry Martens in "The Caring Congregation," says: "But ministry is not the function of a few multi-gifted persons who serve. Rather, ministry is the work of a multi-gifted body intended by God for a priestly ministry. All Christians are servants called to minister to people in need. . . . Care is not the function of an <u>exclusive class</u> of ordained persons who are the designated caregivers of the church" (p. 20).

    Al Dueck in "The Caregiving Team" talks about four types of individuals who give care: (1) Informal Caregivers (spontaneous or self-initiated care in the congregation); (2) Lay/Formal Caregivers (deacons, set aside and trained to give care); (3) Ordained/Formal Caregivers (pastoral care); and (4) Trained Counselors/Caregivers (professional and specialized caregivers). In introducing the need for Lay/Formal Caregivers, he says, "Informal networks do not ensure that the needs of everyone in the congregation will be met" (p. 24).

- Discuss as a group:
    1. How does the office of deacon intersect with Martens' emphasis that the ministry of caring is for all Christians in the church?
    2. In what ways do you agree or disagree with Dueck that each of the four categories of caregivers "plays a very significant role in providing an adequate program of pastoral care for the congregation" (p. 25)?
    3. Does our congregation lean more on the pastor, the deacons, other members, or professional caregivers for meeting spiritual and emotional needs?
    4. Which types of care do we need to encourage, so there is an appropriate balance?

DISCOVERING CARING OPPORTUNITIES

Stressful Events as Caring Opportunities:

• Introduce the following activity as a way to discover opportunities for caring:

When a member of your congregation suffers the death of a loved one, an accident, serious illness, divorce, or other major crisis, the need to reach out becomes an obvious caring opportunity. But what about the many other minor crises of life? A study from the University of Washington identified a variety of stress-producing life events.[3] The study indicated that a significant number of changes in one's life—whether good or bad doesn't really matter—can produce stress which can lead to physical illness or other crisis.

• On the "Life Event Scale" below, check those events you have experienced during the past year. If you have had an experience twice, double its point value. Add all the points and compare your results to the summary scale (given at the end of the list).

The Social Readjustment Rating Scale

Life Event	Mean Value
1. Death of spouse	100
2. Divorce	73
3. Marital separation	65
4. Jail term	63
5. Death of close family member	63
6. Personal injury or illness	53
7. Marriage	50
8. Fired from work	47
9. Marital reconciliation	45
10. Retirement	45
11. Change in health of family member	44
12. Pregnancy	40
13. Sex difficulties	39
14. Gain of new family member	39
15. Business readjustment	39
16. Change in financial state	38
17. Death of a close friend	37
18. Change to different line of work	36
19. Change in number of arguments with spouse	35
20. Major mortgage or debt	31
21. Foreclosure of mortgage or loan	30
22. Son or daughter leaving home	30
23. Change in responsibilities at work	29
24. Trouble with in-laws	29

25. Outstanding personal achievement 28
26. Spouse begins or stops work 26
27. Begin or end school 26
28. Change in living conditions 25
29. Revision of personal habits 24
30. Trouble with boss. 23
31. Change in work hours or conditions 20
32. Change in residence 20
33. Change in schools 20
34. Change in recreation 19
35. Change in church activities 19
36. Change in social activities 18
37. Minor mortgage or debt 17
38. Change in sleeping habits 16
39. Change in number of family get-togethers 15
40. Change in eating habits 15
41. Vacation. 13
42. Christmas. 12
43. Minor violations of the law 11

Using the Scale: 0-150—no significant problems (small chance of illness); 150-199—Mild life crisis (33% chance of illness); 200-299—Moderate life crisis (50% chance of illness); 300 or more—Major life crisis (80% chance of illness).

Life Experiences Related to Caregiving:

• Ask persons to read and reflect silently on the scripture focus given at the beginning of this session (2 Cor. 1:3-4).
    1. Where, specifically, has God, and the people of God, reached out to comfort you in times of trouble?
    2. What implications has your own experience had on your role as a caregiver?

• Break into small groups of three or four persons and ask each person to share in the following ways:
    1. Share briefly a significant need, hurt, or time of stress you have experienced.
    2. In what ways was your need met through the care of others?
    3. Or, what types of caring would have helped you at that time?

- Come back together as a larger group. Name the various opportunities for caring gleaned from your own personal experiences; list these on chalkboard or newsprint. Brainstorm other opportunities for caring and add them to the list.

Hospitality as a Caring Opportunity

- Note whether hospitality was mentioned in your brainstorming of caring opportunities. Then recall a time when you experienced being a guest: as a visitor to a new church, when traveling, visiting in a home, speaking at a church conference. Share a few of these stories in the group, giving special attention to the following:
    1. What kind of hospitality was meaningful to you as a new or lonely person?
    2. How did you feel when someone reached out to you? Or, if they didn't?

- Recall Donald E. Miller's "Deacon Hospitality: A Holy Calling" (p. 63), and discuss the following:
    1. What is the biblical theme that serves as foundation for Miller's article?
    2. Why is the shared meal such an important aspect of hospitality?
    3. What ideas does Miller suggest for ways to make people feel welcome? What ideas can we add?
    4. Which of our present church programs and structures help meet the hospitality needs of new people?

GROUP RESPONSE

- Ask yourselves as a deacon group:
    1. What is the importance of the biblical theme of hospitality, in both Old and New Testaments? How does this instruct our own congregation?
    2. Are there ways we can organize ourselves or the congregation to reach out in meaningful ways to every Sunday visitor? What other persons need hospitality in our congregation or community (students at nearby colleges, new persons in the neighborhood, refugees, persons in sheltered care homes)?

Assignment:
- Assign two or three deacons to bring back to this group an action proposal on hospitality that addresses one of the above concerns.

- Pray together for a clearer awareness of caring opportunities in your congregation.

YOUR PERSONAL JOURNEY

In Your Journal:

- Reflect upon the life stages (changes, challenges, losses) you have already faced and moved through. How do these equip you to comfort and care for others?

- Refer back to the stress scale you took during this session; list current events in your own life which involve changes, challenges, loss. Ask: What emotional or spiritual needs am I experiencing as a result?

- Make a list of five people close to you, including family members, and/or friends, neighbors. Beside each name, write current life events, changes, challenges in that person's life which might present a caring opportunity.

Steps to Take:

- Share with a spouse, friend, or another deacon the emotional and spiritual needs you are currently experiencing. Don't dismiss them as "silly" or "too minor to bother with." Ask that person to pray with you.

- Choose one person listed in your journal and visit, phone, or in some other way reach out in caring. Or. . .

- Invite someone other than a friend to share a fellowship meal with you or your family this week. (Ask a visitor home after Sunday service? Take a new coworker out to lunch? Invite a stay-at-home mother or unemployed person for coffee?)

Preparation for the Next Session:

- Read "Deacons: Channels of God's Healing Spirit" by Joan George Deeter (p. 67).

- Meditate on 1 Timothy 4:12-16.

Session 3
Being There

"Don't let anyone look down on you because you are young, but set an example for the believers in speech, in life, in love, faith and in purity" (1 Tim. 4:12 NIV).

Focusing Your Objective:

To focus on the quality of presence as an important function of being a deacon; to understand the importance of listening as a caring skill; and to explore and apply some basic skills of good listening.

GETTING STARTED

- Ask the persons assigned to work on an action proposal to facilitate hospitality to present their work to the group. Give initial responses, but do not try to work out details at this time.

- Choose a partner and share any caring opportunities you had since the last session. Be sensitive to needs for confidentiality (no names are necessary). What was the hurting person's response? What did you learn?

EXPLORING THE FUNCTIONS OF DEACONS: PRESENCE

Understanding Presence as Caregiving Ministry:
- Share the following incident, reported by R. C. Sproul in his book, *The Holiness of God*:

    A professional golfer was invited to play in a foursome which included Billy Graham. As they came off the round a friend asked the golfer what it had been like. The pro colored the air with curses and fumed, "I don't need Billy Graham stuffing religion down my throat!" He then stormed off to a practice tee where he angrily whacked ball after ball. His friend waited until the pro calmed down and then asked, "Was Billy a little rough on you out there?" The pro sighed, a little embarassed, "No, he didn't even mention religion. I just had a bad round."

    Billy didn't have to say a word to make the pro uncomfortable; he was simply being himself, a man of God. To those who reject God, the presence of Christ in our lives is the "smell of death;" to those who are "being saved," Christ's presence through us is the "fragrance of life" (2 Cor. 2:15-16, NIV).

- Consider Anita Smith Buckwalter's statement, "When our lives embody the gospel in such a way that others notice and are led to the truth, then we are involved in the caring ministry of presence" (p. 75). Then read Buckwalter's story of Bob and Russ (pp. 75-76), and discuss the following:
    1. Bob affirmed the ministry of presence he received from Russ: "It is who you are and that you were there." How did this kind of ministry give Bob the courage to confront his problems?
    2. What other caring functions besides presence did Russ fulfill? How did these work together to support and encourage Bob?

- Read and reflect on the following statements related to the ministry of presence:

    Fred Swartz, in "The Image and Ministry of Deacons Within the Congregation," states, "Deacons thus can be looked to as persons who lead exemplary lives in loyalty to the church and in love and ministry to others. This is not to imply that deacons are set on a pedestal of righteousness, but rather that the church recognizes these brothers and sisters as disciples who are striving to give their best to the service of their Lord and are living out their Christianity from that commitment" (p. 53).

    And Joan George Deeter, in "Deacons: Channels of God's Healing Spirit" says, "We want deacons who are known for the sincerity of their commitment. . . the integrity of their lives. . . an authentic faith, devotion to the church, and a lifestyle respected by others" (p. 67) —in short, "who we are."

    Deeter also expands on the importance of our own life struggles in equipping deacons for caring: "It is not the absence of turmoil that provides the best qualification for ministry; instead, equipping comes as faith is refined in the hot fire of personal agony. Those best able to sympathize with the weakness of others are those who have walked in similar paths." She uses the image from the book of Joel, of the damage that a plague of locusts do when they descend on crops. However, "the year following the visitation of the locusts, the fields now fertilized with the corpses of the locusts produce more than in any other year. And so it is with us; it is precisely our deepest hurts that provide the most solid base for ministry to one another in community" (p. 67-68).
    1. How do these statements speak to you of your ministry of presence as a deacon?
    2. Where do you agree or disagree with these understandings of presence as ministry?

- Divide into small groups of four to six persons. Recall Deeter's stories in which "bridges (were) built through shared pain."
    1. Share similar stories when "shared pain" brought comfort, strength, and healing to you.

2. What questions come to you about the ministry of presence? Write down these questions for sharing with the total group at the end of the session.

DEVELOPING CARING SKILLS: LISTENING

The Importance of Listening:
- Indicate that the ministry of presence includes "being there" for another person. We bring *who we are* to be with the person who is hurting. And learning to listen allows us to be totally present with the other person.

Stumbling Blocks to Listening:
- Indicate that, on the surface, listening seems to be taking place if one person is quiet while another person is talking. But underneath the surface, a number of stumbling blocks may actually be happening. Use two volunteers for the following demonstration of stumbling blocks to listening.
- Ask one person to read aloud the first statement and the other to read the stumbling block (in parentheses). Continue through all the statements:
    1. "Wonder what we're having for supper tonight? . . . Mmm, got to remember to make that phone call . . . " (The "listener" is not really paying attention but is letting her mind wander.)
    2. "Let's see, I'll share my experience along that line, maybe start out like this . . ." (The listener is just waiting until the other person is done so he can say what he wants to say.)
    3. "What is she so upset about? This doesn't seem like a big deal to me . . . (The listener hears the words, but fails to accept the feelings behind the words.)
    4. "What was that? He shouldn't talk about Mr. Smith that way. Got to put a stop to that right now!" (The listener picks up a minor point and responds to that rather than the main point being communicated.)
    5. "I've tried that before and it doesn't work . . . " (The listener is filtering what the other person is saying through his own perspective rather than being objective.)
    6. "I really don't get what he's driving at. Oh, well, guess it doesn't matter. If I don't say anything, maybe it'll just blow over . . . " (The listener doesn't understand what the person is trying to say but lets it go).
- List on chalkboard or newsprint the common "stumbling blocks" you saw here (not paying attention, mind wandering, deciding how to respond, refusal to accept other's feelings . . .).

Principles and Values of Good Listening:
- Remind the group that to listen is to "pay attention in order to hear" what another person is trying to communicate, and that numerous principles for good listening can be found in scripture. Look up the following verses, read them aloud, and make a list of the principles for good listening they

contain: Ecclesiastes 5:1-2; James 1:19; Deuteronomy 1:17; Proverbs 18:15; Matthew 15:10; Proverbs 1:5.

- Share the following. Duane Ewers, in *A Ministry of Caring*, says, "Persons who have been especially helpful to another will often say, 'But all I did was listen.' But think about what good listening can do." Ewers then offers these values of good listening:[4]
    1. Good listening keeps the listener from giving instant solutions.
    2. When a person feels heard, a person feels cared for.
    3. When a person feels heard, a sense of trust develops with the listener.
    4. Good listening encourages a person to talk, and talking often diffuses strong feelings. A person can then focus on dealing with the problem at hand.
    5. Being listened to encourages hope.
    6. When a person feels heard, he or she is more likely to hear and value what the listener says.

Learning to Listen—Two Exercises:
- Divide into small groups of four to six persons. Read aloud each statement below. Listen for (1) *information* that is being shared, and (2) the *feeling* behind the words. After each statement, write a response in your own words; then share your responses. Were some responses more helpful than others? Why or why not? Continue with each statement.
    1. "This is the third time I've been sick this year. I think my health is going downhill. I won't be able to do the things I like to do anymore. I don't want to be a burden on my family."
    My response:

    2. "My boss is really on my case. I don't think I can take it anymore. My wife thinks I should stick it out. But how much should a man put up with?"
    My response:

3. "My son and I are drifting apart. We used to have such good times. But all he wants to do is be with his friends now. I didn't realize the teen years would be like this."
   My response:

4. "Everyone already seems to have their clique of friends. It's very hard to break in. It wasn't this way at the last church I attended. This church really needs to work on this or you're going to lose people."
   My response:

- Use the following exercise if time permits. Pair up in twos. Partner A listens while Partner B shares something about which he or she has strong feelings. At the end of three minutes switch roles, and Partner B listens for three minutes to Partner A. At the end of six minutes, reconvene the group. Each person briefly share an essential fact or feeling learned about his or her partner. (If your group is large, divide into groups of eight or ten persons for the sharing so that everyone has a chance to give feedback.)

GROUP RESPONSE

- Share in the large group the questions about the ministry of presence which were collected in small groups. Respond to each other's questions.

- Ask each other: Are there persons or groups of persons in our congregation who don't feel listened to? (teenagers? handicapped adults? minorities?) Are we listening to their needs and feelings? How can we do this?

Assignment:
- Name caring opportunities where the ministry of presence is needed. Should one or two deacons be assigned to reach out in each situation? If special care is needed, ask for suggested responses from the group before visits are made.

- As time allows, dicuss plans for implementing the proposal for hospitality which was introduced at the beginning of this session.

- Pray together for growth in sensitive listening and for lives that embody the "good news" for others.

YOUR PERSONAL JOURNEY

In Your Journal:
- Meditate on Psalm 116:1-2. To what extent is this true of my relationship with God?
- Think of those who embody God's presence for you. Who *really* listens to me? How do I know this person really hears me? How does it make me feel? Is there someone who by just being who they are has had a deep and positive effect on my life? What encouragement and growth did I experience from this person's presence?

- Reflect on your own ministry as a deacon. What implications does the ministry of presence have for my own life? What caregiving gifts do I bring to caregiving situations? (Don't limit yourself to skills and functions discussed thus far in these sessions. Think broadly.)

Steps to Take:
- Choose a person you may not normally take the time to listen to (the neighbor's child, the receptionist at work, your father). Initiate a conversation, giving opportunity for the person to talk about himself or herself. Listen for new facts and feelings you were not previously aware of.
- Read Henri Nouwen's book, *The Wounded Healer* (see Bibliography).

Preparation for the Next Session:
- Read the following articles:
  "The Annual Deacon Visit: A Form of Pastoral Care" by Karen Peterson Miller (p. 59).
  "Remembering How It Was: An Interview with John Lapp and Clarence Kulp" by June A. Gibble (p. 39).

Session 4
Speaking the Truth in Love

"Brothers, if someone is caught in a sin, you who are spiritual should restore him gently. But watch yourself, or you also may be tempted. Carry each other's burdens, and in this way you will fulfill the law of Christ" (Gal. 6:1-2 NIV).

Focusing Your Objective:
To focus on the discipling function of being a deacon; to grow in the ability to use scripture and prayer in caring for persons' needs; and to practice making caring visits through the use of role play.

GETTING STARTED

- Reflect, as a group, on the various caregiving situations in which you have been involved. What caring gifts were used in these situations? As the group brainstorms, list on chalkboard or newsprint the various caring gifts mentioned. Save for later reference.

- Ask persons to name some feelings about the annual deacon visit from their reading of the interview with John Lapp and Clarence Kulp (p. 39). Also share personal memories of such deacon visits. In what ways were these visits helpful? Not helpful?

EXPLORING THE FUNCTIONS OF DEACONS: DISCIPLING

Discipling through the Annual Visit:
- Indicate some of the many images the discipling function of deacons calls forth: confronting a person on issues of faith and commitment; one-on-one nurturing of a new Christian; discerning the faith response in a crisis situation; shepherding new converts through baptism and membership.

- Read the following statement made by Fred Swartz in "The Image and Ministry of Deacons Within the Congregation," and respond to the questions following: "The deacons can be the most effective group in the church to encourage renewal of faith and participation of those who are separated or inactive members . . . [and] can thus represent a contemporary version of the former annual deacons' visit which challenged people to evaluate their commitment and discipleship for Christ" (p. 53).

1. In what ways has the annual deacon visit been an effective means for discipling?
2. In its decline, what other structures or means for discipling have taken its place (if any)?
3. What would be the most positive aspects of revitalizing the annual deacon visit?

• Read aloud Buckwalter's section on Discipling (pp. 73-74). Discuss:
1. In what way is the function of discipling similar to the function of nurturing as defined by Buckwalter? What distinctions can be made between the two?
2. In what ways do the functions we have explored thus far (serving, nurturing, presence) help prepare the way for discipling?

• Note that in the article, "The Annual Deacon Visit: A Form of Pastoral Care," Karen Peterson Miller acknowledges that this annual visit has declined. Yet she also believes that such a visit can serve an important function in providing an opportunity for members to review "[their] relationship with God and Jesus Christ, as well as [their] relationships within the community of believers" (p. 60).
1. Do you believe that annual deacon visits can care for this function among church members today?
2. What would a renewal of such visits mean for your congregation?

• Read aloud and discuss the following scriptures:
Galatians 6:1-2
1. According to this scripture, what is the goal of confronting a person about his or her sin?
2. Who is supposed to do this? What attitude is to be carried to such a situation?
3. What kind of "burdens" are referred to in this scripture?
4. What is the "law of Christ" that is to be fulfilled?
Ephesians 4:11-16
1. What is the mutual goal of differing ministries, including deacons (vv. 12-13)?
2. In what way does "speaking the truth in love" (v. 15) address the spiritual immaturity described earlier (v. 14)?
3. What forms might "speaking the truth in love" take for the deacon involved in discipling?
2 Timothy 3:14-17
1. What is the "usefulness" of scripture?
2. Why does it have these attributes?
3. What is the goal for using scripture in these ways?

Touching the Spiritual:
- Read aloud the following in the total group:

The love we have to share as Christian caregivers is the love of Christ, which completely embraces the whole person: physical, emotional, mental, social, and spiritual needs. Christ often ministered to a specific need—casting out a demon, healing a blind man, welcoming the children. But he also went beyond the perceived need and touched the deeper spiritual need, as when he forgave the paralyzed man who was let down through a roof by his four friends. Christ was concerned with *wholeness*.

Unfortunately, says Kenneth Haugk in *Christian Caregiving—A Way of Life*, "when people stand in need of care, they often find their needs divided among specialists in caregiving. Physicians seize the physical; psycho-therapists or counselors, the mental and emotional; friends and family, the social. Perhaps the spiritual goes begging for want of a willing caregiver—or it falls squarely on the shoulders of the pastor, whose job description supposedly reads, 'Spiritual Care Provider.' . . . As a Christian caregiver, you continually need to have your eyes open to the spiritual dimension of people's concerns."[5]

- Discuss in small groups of three or four persons each:
    1. What obstacles have you experienced in ministering to spiritual needs in caregiving situations?
    2. What fears or hindrances within yourself have you experienced in touching the spiritual needs of another person?

DEVELOPING CARING SKILLS: USING SCRIPTURE AND PRAYER

- Study the following suggestions from Kenneth Haugk. Read one section and respond to the ideas. Then move on to the next section.

Opening the Door for Spiritual Talk[6]
    1. Provide an atmosphere of acceptance. Listening plays an important role here. As trust develops, people often become more willing to discuss personal spiritual matters.
    2. Be alert to spiritual needs. Develop your ability to discern the hidden cry for spiritual help in a crisis.
    3. Encourage people to discuss spiritual needs. Ask how (this particular crisis) is affecting their view of God, what values are important to them, how they feel about God's care.
    4. Take whatever time is necessary to discuss spiritual concerns. If a person is struggling with faith in the midst of a crisis, he or she may gain new insights into his or her relationship with God if you give adequate time to listen, understand, and discuss.

Pitfalls to Avoid[7]
    1. Avoid preaching. Don't let the discussion become a monologue. Keep the discussion between equals.

2. Avoid religious cliches. "All you need is faith" . . . "Thank the Lord in all things" . . . "Don't worry, God loves you" are shallow, inappropriate responses to difficult life problems.
3. Avoid a know-it-all attitude. You may have strong convictions on certain matters. Feel free to share your insights, but you do not have to justify your beliefs or force your understanding on another.

When to Use Prayer[8]
1. When it's natural. Careful listening will help you discern when prayer is appropriate.
2. Not as an injection. Don't tack prayer onto a visit to make it "Christian."
3. Not as a technique for leaving. You might want to pray with people at times other than the end of a visit.
4. Not as a way to manipulate. Don't talk to God about something you're wanting the person to do or a way he or she needs to change. Pray for the person's expressed needs.
5. Ask if the person would like to pray. Most of the time, your suggestion will be welcome. If the person says no, respect the reason. But if he or she is feeling "unworthy," encouragement might be appropriate.
6. If you're asked to pray . . . Pray simply and honestly; choose meaningful words. Some persons might appreciate one of the Psalms or The Lord's Prayer.

Using Scripture Effectively[9]
1. Why use scripture? It's God's Word to us; it's alive! It addresses a broad range of human conditions and concerns. It contains the promises of God and brings hope.
2. The Bible you use. A small Bible you can slip into pocket or purse is handy. The person you visit may be more comfortable with a certain translation; use it if you can.
3. Knowing passages ahead of time. Begin keeping a list of passages appropriate to different situations as you do your own reading. Ask the people you visit if any verses are especially significant to them; this equips you to be a better caregiver, and allows them to give to you.
4. Introducing scripture. Use scripture that has been meaningful to you. Share the Bible to bring reassurance, to confront when necessary, to deepen understanding, and to strengthen the person's relationship with God in the midst of present circumstances.

Role Playing a Caring Visit:
- Indicate that a role play is a good way to practice caring skills. Divide into groups of three or four persons. Assign different role plays to different groups; if there is time, a group may want to do more than one role play. One (or two) person(s) will be visited; one (or two) will be the visitor(s); one (or two) will be observer(s).

- **Instructions:** Don't pretend that the situation is "real." Rather, "act out" your role. Don't worry about how you are doing, since you can learn from times when things don't go well. If you do more than one role play, switch roles so that each person has the opportunity to be the visitor, the one visited, and an observer.

- **Observers:** Keep back from the role play so you don't become part of the action. Call "time" at the end of ten minutes. Watch for a balance of listening and speaking responses. Was a need identified? Was the response helpful? Were there appropriate opportunities for prayer or use of scripture? Discuss with the "players" what you observed, as well as the thoughts and feelings the participants experienced.

<u>**Care-receiver's Cue Card**</u>   <u>**Caregiver's Cue Card**</u>

Role Play A

You are Ellie Smith, a single parent. You just received a job promotion which will mean some travel. You are worried, however, about the effect on your 14-year-old son, whose grades have been falling and who is spending his time hanging around McDonalds.

You know that Ellie Smith, a single parent, just got a job promotion which will mean more travel. You are also aware that her young teenage son seems sullen and withdrawn. You call her one evening.

Role Play B

You are Linda and Jim Thompson, newlyweds. You, Linda, have three children from a previous marriage. You, Jim, feel awkward with sudden parenthood and intimidated by the children's natural father who takes them on weekends. You are new to the church and shy about making friends.

You recently met Linda and Jim Thompson at church. They have three children who never attend because they are with their natural father on weekends. They both seem quiet. You talk to them after the Sunday service.

Role Play C

You are Bill Brown; you recently lost your job in advertising and have decided to go into business for yourself. You've had to go into debt to launch the business; things are tense at home because your wife Lucy is fearful that you won't make it.

You are aware that Bill Brown has recently gone into business for himself; you have also heard from others that Lucy Brown isn't totally supportive of this direction. She seems anxious and strained. You ask Bill to have coffee.

Role Play D

You are Tom and Sue Daniels, Christians only a short time. You, Sue, recently went back to work full-time; time at home with the children and for housekeeping chores now seems extremely limited and precious. When your sharing group at church reorganized, you simply didn't feel you had the energy to make new friends or give one evening a week. You both now only attend service on Sunday.

Tom and Sue Daniels are neighbors whom you invited to church a year ago. They were converted, baptised, and participated in your sharing group. Sue recently went to work full-time. When your sharing group was reorganized, Tom and Sue dropped out, although they continue to worship Sunday morning. You are concerned about their fellowship and discipleship needs as new Christians. You decide to visit.

- As an alternative to the role play, or in addition, share real-life caregiving situations you are facing. What is the perceived need? What other less visible needs might be present? Brainstorm possible responses. Suggest helpful scriptures.

GROUP RESPONSE

- Respond to this statement by Duane Ewers, writing in *A Ministry of Caring*: "The caring visit is most effective when it is done by one person. Some visitation guidelines suggest that persons go in teams, but visiting a person under stress seems more natural and real when it is done by one person. It is easier for one person to keep the conversation focused. It is easier to share in a more open and honest way with one person. It is easier to develop a sense of trust with one person."[10]
    1. Do you agree or disagree with Ewers about the one-person-visit? Why?
    2. When might the two-person-visit be most appropriate for the one(s) visited? For the ones visiting?

Assignment:
- Consider the broad range of the discipling function: (1) shepherding new converts through baptism and membership; (2) ongoing spiritual nurture; (3) encouraging faith renewal and participation of those who are inactive members; (4) responding to spiritual needs arising from life-stress or crisis situations.

- Ask: What structures do we have in place to respond to these discipling needs? What structures might be useful to give more care to these aspects of the discipling function? How could we revitalize the annual deacon visit to aid the discipling function?

- Form a study group (including the pastor) to evaluate the discipling functions as described above, and make a recommendation to the deacons for meeting these needs.

- Ask one or more professional caregivers from your congregation or another (doctor, nurse, marriage counselor, psychiatrist) to participate in the next session. The Question: How can professional caregivers and informal caregivers in the church support one another in giving optimum care to hurting persons?

YOUR PERSONAL JOURNEY

In Your Journal:
- Do I feel my gifts function best giving care one-on-one? In tandem with another caregiver? In a group setting (such as a discipleship class)? Why?

- In what role do I feel most comfortable: An informal visit to someone in need, as a friend? Or a formal visit on behalf of the church, perhaps one that has been requested? Why?

- In which of the four discipling functions (named above) do I feel I have the most to give? In which functions would I like to receive more training and growth?

Steps to Take:
- Begin a list of scriptures that have been helpful to you and others in various situations: illness, doubt, fear, anger, grief.

- Look for an opportunity to pray with someone who needs spiritual care and support this week.

Preparation for the Next Session:
- Meditate on the following scriptures: 2 Corinthians 5:17-21; James 5:14-16; Isaiah 61:1-3; and Matthew 18:15-20. What kind of healing is implied in each one?

- Reread Deeter's article, "Deacons: Channels of God's Healing Spirit" (p. 67).

Session 5
Healing for Wholeness

"All this is from God, who reconciled us to himself through Christ and gave us the ministry of reconciliation" (2 Cor. 5:18 NIV).

Focusing Your Objective:
    To understand four areas where the healing function of deacons is needed; to explore the complementary roles of caregiving in the church and professional caregivers; and to discover key ingredients in being mediators when relationships are broken.

GETTING STARTED

- Discuss briefly what the concept of healing means to you.
    1. What kinds of healing do you think of?
    2. How do the functions of deacons considered thus far reflect elements of healing?

- Read aloud and give a brief response to Kenneth Haugk's statement on healing: "In the Old Testament the person was viewed as a whole. Brokenness for the Hebrews meant spiritual, emotional, and physical brokenness all at once. The cause and result of all such brokenness was a broken relationship with God. Before healing could take place, the relationship with God had to be restored, or made whole . . . . [On the other hand] peace conveyed the idea of wholeness in relationships, health, welfare, prosperity, and spirit—all of them. The Hebrew word *shalom* . . . means 'peace be with you,' and . . . connotes completeness."[11]

EXPLORING THE FUNCTIONS OF DEACONS: HEALING

Four Areas of Healing:
- Read aloud Buckwalter's section on Healing (p. 73). What four areas of healing are mentioned at the beginning of this section? Write these on chalkboard or newsprint to keep before the group during this session.

- Read aloud and discuss the following scriptures which touch on four areas of healing. Do this in the large group, or divide the scriptures among four groups and report back findings.

James 5:14-16
1. What area of healing is discussed here?
2. What other areas of healing are implied, if any?
3. What steps are taken by the person in need of healing? By the person(s) giving care?
4. What is the response of God the Curegiver?

Isaiah 61:1-3
1. Although many areas of brokenness are mentioned, what primary need for healing underlies them all?
2. What other areas of healing are implied?
3. What actions are taken by the one called to care?
4. What are the results of this healing?

Matthew 18:15-17
1. What is the need for healing discussed here?
2. What action is to be taken by the one who cares?
3. What is the result for the "one who listens," for the caregiver?
4. What is the role of the "one or two others" of the congregation?

2 Corinthians 5:17-21
1. What area of healing is the focus here?
2. Who has initiated steps toward healing (vv. 18-19)?
3. What is our role as caregivers in this healing (vv. 18-20)?
4. What is the healing that takes place (vv. 17-21)?

- After you have discussed all four scriptures, ask:
  1. What role does forgiveness play in each of the areas of healing mentioned in these scriptures?
  2. What are the implications of this for us as Christian caregivers?

Christian Caregiving and the Role of Professionals:
- Ask the professional caregivers you invited to participate in this session to function as a panel and respond to the following questions:
  1. What do you see as the strengths and limitations of professional caregiving (in your particular area)?
  2. What do you see as the strengths and limitations of "nonprofessional caregiving" by deacons or others in the church?
  3. How can we as Christian caregivers support the healing and caregiving that you do?
  4. How can we make use of your resources to help our caregiving be more effective?

DEVELOPING CARING SKILLS: MEDIATION

The Church's Role in Reconciliation:
- Consider Buckwalter's suggestion that, while deacons do not function as professional healers, they can provide an important role in relational and spiritual healing. "The deacons body may function as the congregation's

mediation group, facilitating the process described in Matthew 18:15-20 in conflicts between individuals or groups within the congregation. As non-partisan facilitators, the deacons can help bring about reconciliation and redemption in the conflict situation, preserve the integrity of the church, encourage Christian conduct and attitudes, and nurture loyalty to Christ and the church" (p. 73).

• Lynn and Juanita Buzzard, in *Resolving Our Differences*, suggest three reasons why the church has often failed to get involved in reconciliation: (1) The church has defaulted to secular institutions; (2) the church has defaulted to privatism, rather than community responsibility; and (3) the church is unwilling to risk confrontation; is intimidated by conflict.[12]
    1. Which of these three reasons describe attitudes in our congregation?
    2. Are there other factors which have limited our role as peacemakers and reconcilers among ourselves?

Mediation or Arbitration?

• Read the following, and be sure you understand the difference being made between mediation and arbitration:

"Usually conflict can be dealt with outside formal structures. However, in some cases, the use of formal mediation or arbitration is helpful in creating a structure for resolution . . . . Matthew 18 and 1 Corinthians 6 (re: lawsuits) seem to point toward something like arbitration with the church selecting people to act as arbitrators between disputing parties."[13]

What is the difference, then, between mediation and arbitration? "An arbitrated situation is something like a court situation. The arbitrator is a judge who decides. In mediation, the mediator has no power to decide. Mediators only encourage the parties in coming to a solution."[14]

In their book, *Tell It to the Church*, Lynn Buzzard and Lawrence Eck state, "We must not think of peacemaking as merely a passive or private role. It takes many forms: teaching, preaching, judgment, encouragement, intercession, and advocacy. There are times when those who work for peace will demand that justice be implemented, agreements be kept, and integrity maintained. This role is not really one of mediation or neutrality. The church may use its moral authority, and perhaps its disciplinary structures, to insist that its community accept biblical commands in dealing with disputes.[15]

• Write on newsprint or chalkboard your definitions for both mediation and arbitration. Then discuss:
    1. What kinds of situations seem appropriate for mediation? For arbitration?
    2. What are some of the differences between these kinds of resolutions: justice? forgiveness? reconciliation?

Bringing Hope Through Mediation:
- In *Tell It to the Church*, Buzzard and Eck suggest that the process of mediation might look something like this:[16]
    1. Meet with the concerned parties together (and separately, if it is needed).
    2. Set a spiritual atmosphere. Help the persons involved to avoid competition, retaliation, or coercion.
    3. Get all issues out into the open. Help identify causes.
    4. Assist parties in communicating, sharing, listening to each other. Focus not only on facts, but also on feelings.
    5. Insist on the following rules: (a) no interrupting; (b) each side has its turn to share; (c) be specific.
    6. Look for areas of compromise and suggest alternatives.
    7. Keep the focus on reconciliation, not winning or losing.

- Divide into small groups of four to six persons, and consider the following situations. Read each situation aloud, then discuss the following:
    1. Does this process call for mediation or arbitration? Why?
    2. What would be the best way to initiate a process of reconciliation?
    3. What seem to be the issues here for the persons involved?
    4. What would be the issues for the church, if any?
    5. Does this situation call for justice? forgiveness? reconciliation?

Situation A

Peter and Maggie Conners are a talented couple with a small business. They have an opportunity to expand their operation to make it more versatile; however, they are not able to get another bank loan. An older businessman in the church, Larry Burbank, takes an interest in the Conners and gives them a personal loan of $12,000. The expansion, however, does not go well, and the Conners soon have to shut down the business altogether. They are able to do so without declaring bankruptcy, but they cease making payments on Burbank's loan. Larry asks Peter about the payments several times, and receives assurance that the payments will be forthcoming as soon as the Conners get on their feet. But ten months pass, and still no payments. Yet Larry notices that Peter recently purchased video equipment. Larry is upset because the loan money had come from retirement funds for himself and his wife. He turns to the deacons in the church for help.

Situation B

Deacon Bill Jones has been assigned a new young couple who seem eager to get involved in the church. Lucy and Paul are enthusiastic and volunteer for different service projects, although they have not yet begun a formal membership process. In looking ahead, Bill imagines them as good candidates to take over the junior high youth group when the current leaders phase out at the end of this year. Then Bill hears from an irate member that Lucy and Paul are not married, but have been living together for two years.

This irate church member has already confronted Lucy and Paul about the situation. Bill is taken aback and wonders what to do. He knows the church must address this issue with the young couple, but he doesn't want to lose them unnecessarily.

Situation C

Deacon Sue Brown gets a call from Nancy Thomas, who is upset because her husband Nick left the house after a big fight and has not returned six hours later. He has the car and the checkbook. In the course of the conversation, Nancy reveals that Nick hit her in the face and broke her glasses during the fight. But Nancy says Nick mustn't know she told, because it is a matter of loyalty between them that one doesn't "tell" on the other. At ten o'clock that night, Nancy calls again to say Nick is home, acting like nothing happened. Sue wonders what her responsibility is, knowing something she isn't supposed to know. Should someone confront Nick? Who? What are the consequences for Nancy if someone does? If someone doesn't?

GROUP RESPONSE

- Consider the various roles involved in the healing function: teaching; prayers for healing (public and private); anointing; "being with" persons in their pain; enouraging persons toward wholeness; mediation; professional resources. Are there other roles you see in the healing function?

- Discuss as a total group:
  1. What role(s) should we take as deacons in physical healing? How do we develop these roles effectively?
  2. Are there current situations in our church which call for mediation? For arbitration? Are we prepared to initiate a process of reconciliation? Or do we need teaching to prepare the congregation, and more organization and training to prepare ourselves?
  3. How are we making use of the professional resources among us in our healing ministry? Do we rely on professional resources too much? Not enough?

Assignment:
- Identify a situation in your congregation which needs healing in each of the four areas (physical, relational, emotional, spiritual). In each situation, decide on an initial step which can be taken by the deacon body, by teams, or by individual deacons.

- Pray together for growth in wholeness for each person in the deacon body; for wisdom and courage to minister wholeness to persons in your congregation.

- You may want to assign several persons to do further study in the area of reconciliation. Two helpful books are *Resolving Our Differences* by Lynn and Juanita Buzzard, and *Tell It to the Church* by Lynn Buzzard and Lawrence Eck (see Bibliography).
- Further study on the use of anointing for healing and wholeness can be assigned, if desired. Resources for this include the packet *Anointing* and videotape "Is Any Among You Suffering?" available from Brethren Press (see Bibliography).

YOUR PERSONAL JOURNEY

In Your Journal:
- Reflect in your journal on these questions: In what way(s) have I experienced the healing power of forgiveness (from God; from others; toward others)? Is there an area of brokenness in my life in which I need healing? What first step should I take toward wholeness?

- Ask yourself: in which area of healing do I feel I have the most to give: physical, emotional, spiritual, relational? Why?

- If I had opportunity this week to participate in ministering healing and/or wholeness to a person or situation, describe what happened. What did I learn from this exerience? What questions do I have? What do I feel needs to happen next?

Steps to Take:
- Be alert for areas of brokenness among family members or coworkers. Is there opportunity to pray with this person? To share your own experiences of healing and wholeness? To minister encouragement through touch? To offer Christ's forgiveness? Take the initiative.

Preparation for the Next Session:
- Read the following articles:
  "Elements of a Deacon Training Program by James M. Lapp. (p. 79).
  "Variations in Anabaptist Traditions" by Harold E. Bauman (p. 33).
  The descriptions of congregational deacon ministries in various congregations (pp. 127-150).

- Meditate on Colossians 3:15-17.

Session 6
Keeping the Spirit Alive

"Let the word of Christ dwell in you richly as you teach and admonish one another with all wisdom, and as you sing psalms, hymns and spiritual songs with gratitude in your hearts to God" *(Col. 3:16 NIV).*

Focusing Your Objective:
   To consider briefly the worshipping and advocating function of deacons; to develop our job description as deacons; to consider and plan for ongoing deacon support and evaluation; and to initiate a plan for ongoing training in at least three specific areas.

GETTING STARTED

- Choose a partner and share with each other any personal growth toward wholeness that has happened in your life recently. Affirm that growth for one another.

- Share in the larger group any experiences, informal or formal, where you had opportunity to minister healing to another in one of the four areas: physical, emotional, spiritual, relational. What was most significant to you in the experience?

EXPLORING THE FUNCTIONS OF DEACONS: WORSHIP-PING and ADVOCATING

Worshipping:
- Read aloud Buckwalter's section on Worshipping (p. 74). List on chalk-board or newsprint the various service tasks which historically have characterized this function.

- Discuss both aspects of the worshipping function as given by Buckwalter: leadership in corporate worship and small group or one-to-one worship experiences. How are both important for you as deacons?

- Consider the following:
   1. In what ways does the worshipping function differ from the other functions explored thus far?

    2. How does this function fulfill the definition of the deacon as servant? (Servant to the congregation? To the pastor?)

    3. How are these functions carried at present in our congregation?

- Read Colossians 3:15-17:

    1. What must "rule in (our) heart" as we approach the worshipping function? Why?

    2. What must we allow to "dwell in (us) richly" as we lead out in public ministry or in personal worship ministry? What is the importance of this prerequisite?

    3. What is the significance of Paul's encouragement in each of these three verses to practice thankfulness (gratitude) to God as we minister in both word and deed?

Advocating, Speaking on Behalf of . . .

- Indicate that advocating is the function of deacons which involves (1) speaking on behalf of those who can't speak for themselves, as well as (2) speaking on behalf of the values, teachings, and practices of the church. Then read aloud Buckwalter's section on Advocating (p. 75).

- Read Proverbs 31:8-9 and discuss:

    1. In what ways is advocating inherent in all the functions of deacons? In what ways is this a separate function?

    2. What persons or groups within your congregation might need the voice of an advocate?

    3. Name some of the specific values, teachings, and practices of the church for which you as deacons are advocates, saying "We stand for these values."

    4. Does being an advocate both for persons and groups within the church, as well as for the church itself, imply that deacons should be all things to all persons? If so, how does this make you feel? If not, why not?

DEVELOPING OUR TASK: ONGOING TRAINING, SUPPORT, AND EVALUATION

- Indicate that these training sessions are coming to an end, and your task as deacons is just beginning. These sessions have provided a foundation for caring, exploring the functions of deacons and some basic skills; yet the need for training, support, and evaluation is ongoing. So the last part of this session will be spent laying the groundwork for ongoing deacon ministry in the following areas:

    1. defining your task and writing a specific job description;

    2. developing a structure to provide mutual support and regular evaluation, both for the ministry of the deacon body as a whole and for the individual deacons; and

    3. providing for ongoing training that focuses on areas of specific need in your congregation.

Developing Our Task:
- If you had a clear job description for yourselves as a deacon body, written out before you began these training sessions, then evaluate that job description in light of your study. If there is no job description, then it is imperative that you develop one before bringing this process to a close.
- If you read the descriptions of deacon ministries (pp. 127-150) in preparation for this session, share your reflections in the group.
  1. Is there one congregation's deacon program which seems close to our own congregational situation? What functions or tasks were the focus of this plan?
  2. Were there creative ways of approaching some specific deacon functions and tasks which impressed you? Could these become a part of our own deacon program?
- If your denomination has a statement on the office of deacon, study the tasks and roles as outlined. For instance, one denomination defines the following duties:[17]
  1. Ministry at baptism and assistance with new converts;
  2. Ministry at the love feast and communion;
  3. Ministry to the poor and needy in the congregation;
  4. Ministry to the sick and shut-ins of the congregation;
  5. Ministry of reconciliation and restoration;
  6. Ministry through a shepherding program;
  7. Ministry to the bereaved;
  8. Other ministries.
- Use your denominational statement (or the one above) as a base; brainstorm the tasks and roles of deacons which seem most appropriate to your congregational situation. Ask yourselves: Which ones are immediate priorities? Which ones do you want to grow into? Are there any which do not seem to apply? Are there any which are carried by other persons or roles in the congregation? Are there particular needs in our congregation not covered here? Record your conclusions on a chalkboard or sheet of newsprint.
- Consider the roles and tasks of other leaders in the congregation: pastor; church board; church council; elders; program leaders; small group leaders. Ask yourself: Are there deacon tasks and functions mentioned in this study which are being carried by other servant leaders? (e.g., do elders assist the pastor in spiritual oversight of the congregation or function as leaders of shepherding groups?) Should deacons assist in these tasks? Take on these tasks? Concentrate on other tasks?

Deacon Support and Evaluation:
- Recognize that, as deacons, it is important to meet regularly to organize your ministry, support one another, and provide for regular evaluation. This is not a luxury; it is a necessity!

- Recall the samples of congregational deacon ministries (pp. 127-150). What structures for ongoing support and evaluation seem most helpful? Record your answers on chalkboard or newsprint.

- Review "Elements of a Deacon Training Program" by James Lapp (p. 79). Why are each of these six elements important for you as a deacon? As a deacon group?

- Read and discuss the following:
    1. Regular meetings enable deacons to:
        –organize to perform various tasks and functions;
        –discuss needs and caring opportunities within the congregation;
        –assign persons to meet these needs;
        –share caregiving experiences and get feedback;
        –discover and affirm individual gifts;
        –learn from one another;
        –support one another when discouraged;
        –pray for one another.
    2. Apprenticing allows deacons to:
        –pair a new deacon with a more experienced person;
        –get on-the-job training;
        –provide support and encouragement one-on-one;
        –complement each other's gifts in meeting needs.
    3. Evaluation may include questions such as:
        "How is our ministry as a deacon body going?"
        "What tasks are being covered well? What tasks need more attention?"
        "What is working reasonably well and why? What is not going well and why?"
        "What improvements can we make?"
        "How is your ministry as individual deacons going?"
        "Where have you been effective?"
        "Where would you like to improve?"
        "What kind of support is most valuable to you?"
    4. Keeping a journal allows you to:
        –grow in your own spiritual awareness and faith life;
        –describe caring experiences for later evaluation;
        –record your feelings and questions;
        –keep track of prayer concerns and answered prayer;
        –record personal challenges and growth.

Ongoing Training and Practical Application
- Recognize that as deacons, your caregiving skills will be greatly enhanced as you learn more about the specific needs of persons who need care. This is an ongoing task, underlining the need for ongoing training.

- Some specific training events which you may want to consider are given

here. Read through these suggestions, and then add others to the list:
1. How to minister to those in grief.
2. How to minister to those who are dying.
3. How to make a hospital visit.
4. How to work with inactive members.
5. How to minister to a person going through divorce.
6. How to minister to the unemployed.
7. How to minister to the elderly and shut-ins.
8. How to minister to minorities, refugees, exchange students.
9. How to minister to persons with compulsive addictions.
10. How to minister to persons new to the church and/or community.
11. How to minister to farmers facing foreclosure.
12. How to minister to parents in various stages.
13. How to minister to singles and others who live alone.
14. How to minister to families who have a loved one in prison.
15. How to give help on financial matters (budgeting, financial decision making).
16. How to minister to women and families facing crisis pregnancies.
17. How to minister to those requesting prayer for physical healing.

- Other training events might focus on the personal growth of you, the caregiver. Add other suggestions to this list:
1. Communication skills.
2. Discovering one's spiritual gifts.
3. Cultivating inner spiritual resources.
4. Learning more about forgiveness.
5. Dealing with conflict.

A Training Design for Specific Needs:
- Study the following training design, which can be applied to any specific area (need or problem) you wish to learn more about. This basic design can be used, with adaptations, during regular deacon meetings or in a retreat setting.

Session 1:
1. Ask a resource person to present current background about this need or problem. Include the attitudes of others.
2. Ask willing persons who have suffered this need to share their experiences: what they felt; what they needed; what was said or done by others that was helpful; what didn't help.

Session 2:
1. Ask a professional person(s) who encounters persons with this need to share their experience and suggestions for what is helpful and what is not helpful from nonprofessional caregivers.
2. Explore professional resources within the congregation and/or community, and discuss when they should be used.

Session 3:
1. Share your own stories which touch on this need: your attitudes, questions, fears, experiences.
2. If possible, develop a role play or "situation" and discuss possible responses.
3. Identify persons within your congregation who have this need; discuss helpful ways to respond.

GROUP RESPONSE

Developing Our Task:
- Define your task as deacons and write up (or evaluate) your job description.

- Or assign several persons to write a proposed job description and bring it back to the deacon body.

- Remember that the job description must also be approved by the pastor and church board or council.

Deacon Support and Evaluation:
- Decide as a group on the following plan of action:
  1. A time to meet regularly as a deacon group.
  2. Whether to "team" new deacons with experienced persons. (If so, make assignments now? Or next meeting?)
  3. How and when evaluation should take place.
  4. Journaling: Is this a personal decision? Or a group commitment?

Ongoing Training and Practical Application:
- Initiate a plan for additional training, following these steps:
  1. Identify three areas of need in your congregation where you as a group of deacons feel you need specific training.
  2. Discuss the feasibility of doing this training during regular deacon meetings, and/or in a retreat setting.
  3. Decide on tentative dates to do this training in the coming year.
  4. Ask for volunteers (or assign three different persons) to plan each training session, obtain resource persons, etc. Plans should be reviewed with the pastor or the deacon body.

- Spend time in prayer together, thanking God for the growth that has occurred during these training sessions and asking God's guidance on the ongoing ministry of deacons in your congregation.

YOUR PERSONAL JOURNEY

In Your Journal:
- Given the training and experiences of caregiving during these six sessions, which caring gifts do I seem to have? What are my greatest strengths? My limitations?

- In which deacon functions do I feel most called to serve? Which area(s) will be the greatest challenge?

- What kind of support do I need and want as a deacon?

- What are the growing edges for me in relating to this group of deacons? In relating to the congregation? In relating to hurting persons?

Notes

1. Kenneth C. Haugk, *Christian Caregiving—A Way of Life* (Minneapolis: Augsburg Puplishing House, 1984), pp. 40-41.

2. Ibid., pp. 19-20.

3. J. H. Holmes and R. H. Rahe, "The Social Readjustment Rating Scale," *Journal of Psychosomatic Research,* Volume 11, (1967), pp. 213-318.

4. Duane A. Ewers, *A Ministry of Caring—Participant's Workbook* (Nashville: Discipleship Resources, 1983), p. 10.

5. Kenneth C. Haugk, *Christian Caregiving—A Way of Life* (Minneapolis: Augsburg Publishing House, 1984), pp. 50-52.

6. Ibid., pp. 54-58, adapted and summarized.

7. Ibid., pp. 58-60.

8. Ibid., chapter 13.

9. Ibid., chapter 14.

10. Duane E. Ewers, *A Ministry of Caring—Participant's Workbook* (Nashville: Discipleship Resources, 1983), p. 19.

11. Kenneth C. Haugk, *Christian Caregiving—A Way of Life* (Minneapolis: Augsburg Publishing House, 1984), pp. 62-63.

12. Lynn and Juanita Buzzard, *Resolving Our Differences* (Elgin, IL: David C. Cook Publishing Co., 1982), p. 16.

13. Ibid., p. 19.

14. Ibid.

15. Lynn R. Buzzard and Lawrence Eck, *Tell It to the Church* (Carol Stream, IL: Tyndale House Publishing, 1985).

16. Adapted from *Resolving Our Differences,* p. 20.

17. *The Office of Deacon,* Church of the Brethren Annual Conference Statement, 1983. Available from Church of the Brethren General Board, 1451 Dundee Avenue, Elgin, IL 60120.

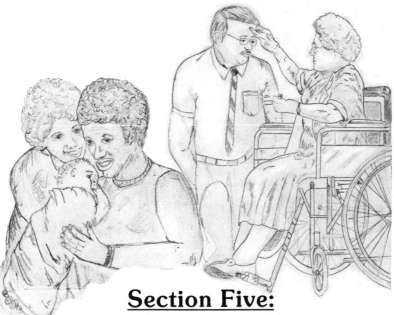

Section Five:
Samples of Congregational Deacon Ministries

People Centered Deacons

Ambler Congregation
Ambler, Pa.

The nineteen deacons, nine married couples and one whose spouse is not a deacon, of the Ambler Church of the Brethren, tend to be a relaxed group, laughing with each other, studying, praying, and working together with obvious enjoyment. They enjoy their work especially when (a) they know what they are doing, (b) they feel well prepared, and (c) they have clear assignments.

Through their own lay initiative they have developed challenging goals, effective procedures (always subject to evaluation and re-formation), and clear outlines of responsibility as they discharge their "people caring" mandate.

Purpose and Goals for the Deacons

The minutes of the Ambler deacon board for the past ten years show significant efforts to restate the ways to fulfill the bylaw goal of "assisting the pastor in a program of evangelism, visitation, and anointing." One of the documents called for:

1. creating a caring community, responsive to the hurts and needs of people (including spiritual, mental, and physical needs);
2. helping to create an open fellowship, welcoming the visitor, and encouraging commitment, growth, and development in church membership;
3. enabling men and women to articulate their Christian faith, to experience the grace of forgiveness and reconciliation, and to develop a Christian life style of peace, good will, and service;
4. cooperating with the pastor in services of Love Feast, baptism, spiritual nurture programs, anointing service, baby dedication.

Someone added, "and to become the 'eyes and the ears' in respect to the needs of the congregation."

Election and Organization

The deacons are elected as a husband and wife team or as an individual for a five year term. They may succeed themselves by election. They are elected directly by the Church Council (the entire membership) through a secret write-in ballot.

The deacons organize themselves for the purpose of giving effective care for the individuals and family units of the congregation. They divide the congregation into geographic groups of about ten households per deacon unit. The "household" may be a single person or a multi-generation family. Each deacon is given detailed instruction regarding the assessment of needs and the making of reports to appropriate offices or persons.

The work of the deacons is coordinated with the general program of the congregation through two means: (1) five members are selected to serve on the board of administration of the church, and (2) the chairperson of the deacons is a member of the executive committee of the board.

Activities

At least once a year the deacons plan a concerted effort to contact every family in the congregation. This becomes part of the updating of the membership and attendance and is a source of insight into the experience and development of the individuals and families.

The deacons may select a single focus or a group of emphases for a particular annual visit. One year, the focus (for visits the month before the fall Love Feast) was to involve persons in creating the "spiritual atmosphere" of the church. To prepare themselves, the deacons worked through methods of relating to the various individuals and families in a natural manner. They wanted to make it easy for people to talk about themselves and the church. Through role playing and other methods they learned ways to turn negative ideas that might emerge into constructive criticism. They developed suggestions for encouraging study, worship, and fellowship leading to covenant renewal for spiritual growth and church participation.

In their training sessions, the deacons recognize the differences among the individual deacons in respect to home visits. Some obviously are more at ease and more experienced than others. The deacon body operates with a healthy flexibility while holding one another accountable for accomplishing the job.

One year the deacons promoted a 20-hour training program in caring called "Caritas" conducted by the family counseling organization, Reach Associates, whose offices are located in the church. Each year the deacons plan one or two major spiritual development programs for their own enrichment, and often they open these experiences to the congregation.

Concerns for People

The concerns that catch the eye of the deacons are wide ranging: new-comers moving into the communities; physical needs of particular families, such as unemployment and money shortage; families needing very particular help (such as household moving when the congregation's "Dunkard Moving Service" is available to help); persons struggling with precarious health, forms of buried hurt, or anger that hold them back from full participation; stifling burdens on the job or at home; people lonely or discouraged or depressed; families with two or more religious backgrounds or with persons of no religious interest; problems of alcoholism or drug abuse; destructive relationships within the families; deaths in the family of origin or in extended families; problems stemming from the natural transition periods in family life.

The deacons also watch for occasions of celebration in family life: promotions, graduations, new ventures, travel, awards, accomplishments, new hobbies or activities, engagements and marriage, continuing education programs.

The report program of the deacons provides channels when pastoral calls are needed, when practical help is called for, when items need to be carried in *Grace Notes* (the monthly newsletter), when knowledgeable lay persons in the congregation can help, or when benevolence funds are called for. (The deacons administer the Benevolence Fund which is maintained from Love Feast and communion offerings.) All information about the needs and struggles of individuals or families is treated with strictest confidentiality.

The deacons have developed a prayer chain for alerting the congregation to particular prayer needs. Each deacon has a chart with instructions for the sequence of telephone calls to be made. The prayer chain is activated when there is some form of tragic occurrence, when there are unusual burdens to be borne, in instances of sudden death, or whenever the person or persons concerned and the deacon request such particular spiritual support.

Planned Preparation

The deacons like to be prepared for special occasions such as Love Feast and baptism or other special programs or events. An example is the assignment sheet in connection with a recent Love Feast. The assignments, with regular "time-off" periods built in, rotate the tasks among the deacons; assignments include: The Service Planning, Bread Baking and Food Preparation, Set-up of Tables and Chairs, Setting the Tables, Food and Supply Purchases, Worship Center, Feet Washing Preparations, Greeters/Ushers, Baby Sitters, Laundry, Clean-up Chores. Similiar lists are made for baptismal services. The rotation and "time-off" periods are not only for ease of getting tasks done, but in order to give each deacon the experience of viewing and feeling the different aspects of the services, including unassigned participation.

Membership Responsibility

The deacons interview and recommend prospective members (following the usual "pastor's class") and they recruit and train sponsors for each new member and prepare the congregation-wide welcome lunches for them. The deacons keep the membership records for the congregation. When longterm drop-outs occur, the deacons write friendly letters urging participation and, with gentleness, remind them that names are eventually dropped when there is no response.

In Summary

The deacons of the Ambler congregation carry their responsibilities with skill and good humor. They constantly work at keeping the monthly meeting down to a reasonable length of time, vigorously commending their chairperson when a meeting called at 7:30 adjourns as early as 10:00! One agenda included: Review of Minutes, Report of Benevolence Fund, Pastor's Report, Report of Memorial Service Lunches, Distribution of Morning Worship Tapes for Shut-ins, Report on Deacon Election Criteria, Report of Candidates for Baptism, Review of Responsibility List Visits, Requests for Financial Assistance, Review of Love Feast Assignments, Needs of Particular Persons, and "Other."

The deacons at the Ambler Church of the Brethren are a wholesome, growing, interesting, enjoyable group engaged in ministering in Christ's name. They constitute a strong cooperative team of ministry with the pastoral staff.

—Lynn Leavenworth

A Ministry of
Mutual Accountability

**Chiques Congregation
Manheim, Pa.**

While in years past the main responsibility of the deacons at the Chiques Church of the Brethren was carrying out church discipline, a subtle shift in purpose has occurred. "The shift is away from matters of discipline and reconciliation and more into the area of fellowship concerns—trying to encourage people to be active in the church," explains J. Becker Ginder, one of seven ministers serving this free ministry congregation in Lancaster County, Pa. "The office is conforming to the expectations of the congregation. The congregational life has changed, and in that process the role of the deacons has changed."

But the form of the deacon program has remained traditional Brethren to the core. Deacons are still called by open election without nominations. According to 1 Timothy 3:10, deacons are "tested" for one year before being installed to serve a lifetime. Currently 14 couples serve as deacons for the 526-member congregation, but the number varies according to needs. Becker explains, "If the deacon board itself feels the work isn't getting done, they call for more help. It's really a matter of sensing needs."

Qualifications of a deacon, as outlined in 1 Timothy 3, are not taken lightly. "Our deacons carry responsibility for the spiritual leadership of the church—almost as assistants to the ministers in spiritual matters," says Becker. The deacons "model the Christian faith" for the rest of the congregation. "I think the ministers and the deacons in the free ministry are expected to be the ones who model the faith," says Becker, "the deacons particularly because they're set apart, but yet they're not [set apart]."

He is quick to emphasize that even though more is not expected of deacons than of other members, expectations of deacons are high. Ron Strickler who, along with his wife, Judy, was called to be a deacon four years ago, admits that he senses the high expectations people have of deacons at Chiques, but he doesn't think they are too high. "Expectations should be strong for any Christian," says Ron, "whether a deacon or not. It's a challenge to fulfill the expectations people have of us."

Ron says, "My role is to serve the congregation in the sense of being a helper and a friend." Responsibilities of deacons include preparing and administering the Love Feast and baptismal services, serving on the church board, administering the congregation's benevolent fund, and conducting the annual deacon visits.

Deacons visit each member of the congregation annually and ask members to share feelings about the life of the congregation, make suggestions for the betterment of the church, and respond to three questions: (1) Are you still in the faith of the gospel as you declared in your baptism? (2) Are you, as far as you know, in peace and union with the church? and (3) Will you still labor with the Brethren for an increase of holiness both in yourself and others? Each deacon couple visits approximately 20 families during a seven-week period at the beginning of the year, and then reports results to the deacons and ministers on the church board.

Though the annual deacon visit has been part of Chiques since the congregation's birth in 1868, the tone and purpose of the visit has changed. Becker recalls with a smile, "A few years ago you were notified in advance that the deacons were coming and you got dressed up for it. You went and sat in the living room . . . and sat up straight! As a little kid you were half afraid. Now that is gone." Visits are much more relaxed and enjoyable.

In the past, responses to the three questions were a test of membership, and people felt threatened by the deacon visit, says Becker, but that's no longer so. "The encouraging thing about the visits," he says, "is that instead of putting people on the defensive, they are encouraged to be involved." Each member is given the opportunity to suggest queries to be brought to the next congregational business meeting.

"I think [the deacon visit] lets people know—especially those who aren't very active—that we are still concerned about them," says Ron. "We have them on the roll and we don't just forget about them. We do want to know where they stand with the church. And those people who do come every Sunday, it gives them the opportunity to express their feelings."

Although the emphasis of the annual visits has shifted from assessment and discipline to getting people involved, Becker still sees the deacon visit as a means of holding members accountable to the church: "The idea of accountability is very much there," he says. "There are still some people who say, 'I can't answer those questions because I know that I'm not living up to them.' A person like that is sensing that the expectation of the church is still there—that tension between what is and what ought to be."

If a member does say "no" to any of the questions, the deacon reports back to other deacons and ministers, and a follow-up visit is arranged to see what can be done to rectify the situation. In most cases, however, members respond affirmatively. "If the person answers the questions affirmatively, even though we would have good reason to believe they are not answering truthfully, we believe that it is not our role to judge," says Becker. "That 'goes with them.' "

In recent years deacons have been encouraged to look after their assigned members throughout the year in a kind of undershepherd program. One of the major strengths of the deacon program at Chiques, says Becker, is the way it offers "an opportunity for a significant kind of involvement. We have capable people who are called to special work," he says. "And it's not make-believe. It's very real, and it is a lifetime responsibility. It multiplies the arms of the church; we have more people doing the kinds of things that would be involved in pastoral ministry."

Deacons, along with ministers, also make up the congregation's official board. In the past it was only the male deacons who served on the board, but women now participate in some meetings, and are becoming increasingly active as deacons. Though the structure of the church board is unusual—a carryover from earlier days—Becker sees strength in it. He sees the church board as a stabilizing force, but admits that it is important for older deacons to relinquish leadership roles so that younger ones can step in.

Ron, on the other hand, sees a potential for stagnancy and questions whether the qualifications for a deacon are the same as for a board member. "The deacons that get elected at our church are good people," he says, "but I'm not sure they're the ones who are most qualified to serve on the church board. The weakness I see is that dual responsibility." Becker also sees the need for periodic evaluation of the overall deacon program in order to keep it tuned in to the needs of the congregation.

But the deacon program at Chiques works, and works well. It invites deacons to take a significant leadership role in the congregation. Through the annual visits members are encouraged to stay active and, at the same time, are held accountable to one another. It's a style of deacon program the Brethren have known for many years. And at Chiques it still works.

—Don Fitzkee

An Undershepherd Plan
That Works

Coventry Congregation
Pottstown, Pa.

The members of the Deacon Board at Coventry Church of the Brethren see themselves as a part of the "called-apart" ministry of the church, offering themselves in a lifetime commitment of service according to the gifts they can bring to the group. The deacon body has as its central interest the physical and spiritual needs of the congregation's members. Its program functions under the umbrella of the Undershepherd Plan.

The Undershepherd Plan at Coventry

To carry out the work of the deacon ministry, our deacons are organized under the Undershepherd Plan, concerned with getting each member involved in some form of church activity. The undershepherd program assures members that they are a very important and precious part of the church family, and that the church has an interest in them as they travel their spiritual journey. The undershepherd program works to develop a Christian fellowship that will encourage members to grow in their relationship with the Lord.

The Undershepherd's One-To-One Relationship With The Flock

Each member of the congregation is bonded in a fellowship of love with an undershepherd who shares a like fellowship of love with the flock. Each undershepherd has committed his or her life to personally become involved with the flock's concerns or desires when problems arrive or when there are joys to be shared, thus forming a support system for each member as it is needed. The undershepherd prays for the flock daily and encourages the flock to reciprocate. Daily devotional material is personally handed to each flock member on a quarterly basis, thus opening doors of communication and opportunities for sharing between the undershepherd and his or her flock member.

The Undershepherds' Functioning as a Group

The undershepherds minister to special needs within the congregation, such as emergencies, death, illness, hospitalization. This work is organized through the following committees under the direction of the Deacon Board.

1. The Ministry of Undershepherds
   a. Organizes the undershepherd program.
   b. Assigns undershepherds and their flocks.
2. The Funeral Committee
   a. Gives spiritual support and nurture to grieving families.
   b. Plans and prepares a luncheon for families following the funeral service.
3. Ministry to New Members
   a. Keeps in touch with new members and their sponsors to help the new members find their niche in a compatible church group of their choice where they can continue to grow.
   b. Makes arrangements in conjunction with the Spiritual Nurture Commission for a church reception dinner where new members are welcomed and opportunity is given for new members and congregation to get to know each other.
4. Ministry to the Lonely, Elderly, and Bereaved
   a. Works out the "Keep in Touch" sheet which lists members of the congregation needing nurturing. Names are listed in the following categories: (1) Dear ones in nursing homes, (2) Those confined at home, and (3) Older folks who enjoy and deserve visitors.
   b. Schedules monthly assignments to each committee member and prepares the calendar for plans to visit and who is to visit them.
   c. Keeps a record of those visited to be reviewed later. This is a way of assuring all get visited each month.
5. Ministry of Outreach to the Poor and Needy
   This group meets the needs of those having temporary hardships and consists of two sources of help:
   a. The Helping Hand Fund to help those persons who are within the church family.
   b. The Dee Wampler Fund to help those outside the church but in the local community.
6. Ministry of Prayer and Nurture
   a. Keeps a current list of those willing to pray and forms a united prayer nucleus for those requesting it.
   b. Operates a telephone chain so that the prayer chain can function at any moment.
7. Ministry of Spiritual Enrichment and Evangelism
   a. Makes follow-up calls to visitors to the morning church service.
   b. Makes visits to new families moving into the community.
8. Ministry of Greeting and Fellowship
   a. Makes arrangements for greeters to be at each door of the sanctuary and educational building before and after each morning service.

9. Ministry of Visitation to Other than the Elderly and A Service of Love
   a. Arranges visits to the hospital, to new parents, newlyweds, inactive members.
   b. Sends casseroles into homes as need arises (moving, bringing home a new baby, illness in the family).
   c. Dial-A-Deacon Service—member's direct access to deacon service.
10. Baptismal Committee
    a. Prepares all physical arrangements for the baptismal service.
    b. Deacons selected to be sponsors for persons being baptized will get acquainted with the persons before the day of baptism, welcoming them and beginning a one-to-one caring relationship; the purpose is to ease new members into the fellowship, encourage involvement, find meaningful activities within the church to offer them, call on them at home, and offer guidance as needed.

The Deacon Board—An Observation

Deacons, along with the ministers, make up the congregation's Deacon Board. Both men and women are active participants in the group. This very sharing, open, cooperative group is eager for challenges. The chairperson becomes the representative and liaison to the Church Board of Administration where he or she is an active voting member.

The Deacon Board meets quarterly to plan for future and new avenues of service. Follow-up reports by committee chairpersons keep all deacons on the board aware of the progress and effectiveness of the current program. The congregation is kept aware of the deacons' services available to them through articles printed in the church newsletter.

The deacon program at Coventry is working well for us. It is positively structured with a scriptural and spiritual approach. Deacons are enthusiastically involved. Members of the congregation are responding well to the personal attention given to them. The Spirit of God is moving in our midst. The deacon program at Coventry is like the field of the church at large—"white unto harvest." It is a joy to be serving in the capacity of "gathering in" the flock.

—Hazel Dick, LaVerne Bealer,
John D. Hostetter, Betty Malenke

Meeting Needs Through Deacon Care Groups

**Faith Congregation
Newton, Kan.**

Faith Mennonite Church began as a relatively small congregation where members all knew each other and were usually aware when someone was ill or in need of special ministry. Many of the members participated in small groups within the church. As the congregation increased in size, there developed an awareness of the need for a more structured way to assist the pastor in caring for the needs of members. The Deacon Board, which had been expanded to 12 members by a constitution revision, was aware of "shepherding" programs in other congregations. It was felt that caring for the needs of members was a major responsibility of the deacons and, therefore, should not be delegated to others. Assignment of the total resident membership was made, with approximately ten family units to a deacon.

An attempt was made to have several families of the same general age in the same deacon care group, largely for the sake of the children; but each group included a wide range of ages. This resulted in a diverse group both in terms of age and interest. For some people, this is seen as an advantage, providing a way of learning to know people who would otherwise remain relative strangers. For others, not having anyone they relate to in other settings gives an unnatural feeling to the deacon care group.

The pattern of relating to persons in a particular deacon care group is left up to each deacon. The church office informs the deacon when someone in his or her group has a special need. When appropriate, that information is shared with others in the group. In every group there are individuals who do not enjoy or cannot participate in group activities, but who still appreciate contact by the deacon.

In the first years of the program, meeting as groups was somewhat inconsistent. Eventually it was decided to designate the second Sunday of each quarter for deacon care groups to meet, so that everyone would be aware of the date and other congregational events would not be scheduled. Meeting only once a quarter is a disadvantage for the formation of cohesiveness in the groups. Some have suggested meeting on at least a monthly basis.

Agendas for some of the meetings are proposed by the Deacon Board, or even the Church Council. These have included discussing how to get more participation in the church and whether to hold two worship services on Sunday; how to maintain close ties among church members; pastor/congregation review; and gift discernment. This has allowed more people to feel involved in discussion of congregational matters. However, some of the people would prefer that the deacon care groups be more of a social nature rather than a sounding board for "church business."

Meeting in homes seems to be more conducive to good group dynamics, even though some members' homes can not accommodate a large group. I discovered that the children especially look forward to the meeting in our home, which had become a familiar place.

Discussion continues as to whether the groups should be headed by deacons. Several methods have been suggested for sub-dividing the leadership. Up to now, it has been felt that since concerns of individual members are shared in meetings of the Deacon Board, having non-deacons as leaders of the groups would make the sharing of that information more difficult. At the same time, finding persons who are willing to take on the task of being a deacon is difficult because of the responsibility of deacon care groups.

—Norma Wiens

An Effective Deacon Program in a Small Church

Heatherdowns Congregation
Toldeo, Ohio

Probably the finest attribute of the deacon body of the Heatherdowns Church of the Brethren, with a membership of 85, is the ability of those deacons to fill any gap, including filling the pulpit, as occasion demands.

Our deacons are truly the backbone of our congregation. They are fully involved in the life and activities of the church, faithful in attendance, and responsible far beyond their assigned duties. Whatever the problem or need, one or more will volunteer to see that assistance is provided. Whether participating in the ordinances and worship services, visiting the ill and shut-ins, providing gentle guidance for our children or long term support for the retarded and infirm, or being there for those experiencing grief, these deacons work together well. Extremely flexible, they will pitch in to do unforseen or unassigned tasks—shoveling snow after an early Sunday storm, for example, or providing a meal after a funeral.

The pastors of Heatherdowns, when absent, know that the deacons are able and willing to respond to any eventuality. Their smooth operation leaves an impression of uninterrupted flow of events. And yet these folks are not "doers of the word" only. They are keenly aware of their need for Christ in their lives. By their humility they gently keep the rest of us reminded of our need, as well.

Organization

There are twelve active deacons at Heatherdowns, six women and six men (not all are couples, each being elected on his or her own merit), plus two emeritus women. Chairmanship rotates alphabetically by last names, for one year terms; and monthly meetings follow a Sunday morning worship service, with each deacon bringing a sack lunch. Usually several people bring something to share as well.

Except for the Undershepherd Program, organization is informal. A skeleton agenda, following a devotional period, helps to guide discussion; each person is free to offer observations or concerns which need attention. Agenda topics might include regularly scheduled communions or Love Feasts, baptisms and anointings as appropriate, or support needs within the congregation or without.

Undershepherd Program

The Undershepherd Program at Heatherdowns is carefully structured to be sure that every person associated with the congregation is assigned to a deacon. Each deacon, then, assumes the responsiblity of maintaining contact with the persons on his or her list. "Contact" can mean personal visits, telephone calls, Sunday morning conversation and interaction, cards or notes—whatever seems appropriate to each situation.

One very important means of contact is via the Prayer/Information Line. When it is necessary to disseminate prayer requests, information regarding changes in programming due to weather, or other urgent messages, the deacons are responsible for calling persons on their lists. At times a deacon will request that someone on his or her list call one or more others on that list. If a deacon is out of town or otherwise unable to make calls, the others divide up that list.

Because of the deacons' close involvement with persons in the congregation, it is not often that a need is overlooked. In conjunction with the pastors, they are unobtrusively facilitating the development of a truly caring congregation, as others also become more sensitive to and concerned about each other and more open to outreach emphases.

—Florence and Glen Crago

Organized for a Caregiving Ministry

**Manassas Congregation
Manassas, Va.**

The Deacon Board at Manassas Church was revitalized in 1984 following a study of the 1983 Annual Conference Statement on the Office of Deacon by the congregation's executive committee. Thirty-three new deacons were called, a number deemed sufficient to begin a shepherding program.

The deacons meet quarterly and have divided into five sub-committees to accomplish the ministry assigned them by the congregation's by-laws. Theirs is primarily a caregiving ministry. Consequently, the deacon board does not take a role in directing the congregation's program, although several persons elected to the church board are also deacons.

The deacon sub-committees and their responsibilities are as follows:

Baptism and New Member Committee
(Ministry at Baptism and Assimilation of New Members)
1. Make physical preparations/arrangements for baptismal service:
   a. Launder robes,
   b. Provide floor cover,
   c. Supplemental cleaning of baptistry and area, if needed.
2. Secure deacons to assist baptismal applicants in preparation for baptism, exiting and entering baptistry, dressing, etc.
3. Discuss ways that new members can be encouraged to take an active part in the congregation.

Love Feast and Communion Committee
(Ministry at Love Feast and Communion Services)
1. Secure and maintain a list of deacons with responsibility to:
   a. Prepare meal for Love Feast,
   b. Set up the fellowship hall (tables, chairs, tubs, candles, etc.),
   c. Make the communion bread,
   d. Secure the grape juice,
   e. Dismantle and clean up fellowship hall, kitchen, etc.
2. Assist the pastor by securing deacons to *serve* the communion elements for bread and cup communions (14 servers needed).
3. Evaluate the Love Feast and communion service and make suggestions to the pastor and other appropriate boards/officials on making these services enriching, worshipful experiences.

4. Discuss ways to encourage participation in Love Feast and communion (e.g. attractive invitations to Love Feast sent to all members).

Crisis Support Committee
(Ministry to the Sick, the Shut-ins, the Bereaved, the Victims of Tragedies)
1. Maintain a list of those deacons who are comfortable assisting the pastor with the anointing service and/or officiating at the anointing in the pastor's absence.
2. Prepare a schedule for the Deacon of the Month ministry and determine specific responsibilities of the Deacons of the Month.
3. Design and coordinate a plan whereby the deacon body can give or secure supplemental pastoral care, such as visitation, support to relatives, monetary assistance, etc., to those ill, shut-in, bereaved, or victims of tragic circumstances (fire, flood, accident, etc.) Such a plan should utilize the shepherding program.
4. Assist the congregation's Hospitality Committee in arranging for food and lodging whenever needed in cases of major illnesses, accidents, deaths, etc.

Shepherding Program Committee
(Ministry Through a Shepherding Program)
1. Determine the most practical method for dividing the congregation among the 17 shepherding teams.
2. Discuss what training is necessary and helpful for the shepherds and arrange for such.
3. Reassign or make new assignments of families to shepherds as the need arises (or determine the method to be used for doing so).
4. Devise a way for reporting to be made and important information recorded as a result of the shepherds' care and contacts.

Membership Cultivation Committee
(Evaluation of Spiritual Life and Active Participation of Members)
1. Conduct an annual review of the membership roll of the congregation and determine which members are active and which are inactive. This is done in consultation with the pastor, and is reported to the Congregational Business Meeting in the spring of each year.
2. Suggest ways by which the congregation can minister to inactive members and encourage their participation in the church.
3. Consider (and plan for, if desirable) periodic retreats or meetings to enhance the *spiritual* growth of the congregation. Such events are in addition to and significantly different (in scope, purpose, etc.) from current programs of the church (such as People of the Covenant, School of Christian Growth, etc.).

—Fred W. Swartz

Ministry Through Deacon Care-Groups

**Mountville Congregation
Mountville, Pa.**

Bruce Larson, interviewed for an article in the *Leadership* journal (Fall 1984), described the church as a lonely place for some people. He went on to say, however, that loneliness is a gift. "Loneliness is the psychic pain that drives us to do something about our isolation. God has made us for intimacy. It's not our idea. He put within us a desire to belong to other people . . . I would never risk sharing myself with somebody else unless I was driven to it by my pain. I can't bear to be cut off anymore, so I finally open up in a small group or to an individual. Loneliness becomes the very ground of intimacy"(p.15).

If Larson is correct, and my experience with congregations over the past 20 years tells me he is, the church needs to find creative ways to deal with that reality. Writing to the same concern, Arthur G. McPhee says in *Friendship Evangelism* that "Most men and women are not looking for religion, nor do they often perceive themselves as miserable sinners in need of forgiveness. But most men and women *are* looking for love" (p.56). In other words, most people are looking for caring relationships where they can be honest, feel accepted, and grow as persons and as believers. Can the church respond to this need?

For the past 20-25 years, the Church of the Brethren has worked at meeting this need through the Undershepherd Plan, with varying degrees of success. In my experience with several congregations, I have never seen a truly effective undershepherd program. While some forms of caring ministry do occur in that program, the Undershepherd Plan usually organizes groups that are much too large for caring to happen as described by Larson. At Mountville, the typical Undershepherd Plan would place no fewer than 20 families in a group headed by a deacon team.

In an attempt to organize our program of lay ministry into smaller units, we went one step beyond the Undershepherd Plan. We have nine deacons at Mountville—four husband/wife teams and one single deacon. Therefore, we started with the establishment of *five* Friendship Groups (comparable to undershepherd zones). Each of the four teams was assigned a Friendship Group with a membership of approximately 25 families. The single deacon was given a group about half that size. We then subdivided each Friendship Group into small Care-Groups. We have a total of 13 Care-Groups, and each of those is coordinated by two persons (mostly husband and wife teams, but not in all cases) who are not members of the deacon body. Consequently, we have a care-ministry program that involves a total of 35 lay persons—nine deacons and 26 non-deacons. We think that is a significant number of persons who are directly involved in just one of the many programs in a congregation with 227 members.

We organized the Care-Groups through sign up sheets, where each individual had the opportunity to express a first choice from a long list of possible interests and/or fellowship activities. A steering committee then met to organize the groups, making every effort to bring together persons who expressed common interests. Those who did not express an interest were assigned to a group. In addition, all shut-ins and non-resident members were placed in groups. As a result, every person on the active membership list is assigned to a small Care-Group. The steering committee, as part of the planning process, invited a large number of potential coordinators for the groups to meet for an afternoon of orientation and training, and from that experience the 26 coordinators for the 13 Care-Groups were selected and given their group assignments.

To assist the deacons and the coordinators of the Care-Groups with their ministry, the steering committee prepared a care-ministry "cookbook" which stated the purpose of the program, discussed the matter of accountability, described the role/function of the deacons and coordinators, and gave helps about scheduling the first meeting and the subsequent ministry in each group.

Our program of care-ministry at Mountville has a ten-fold purpose:
1. To enable persons to get together intentionally for fellowship, study, prayer, and Christian service;
2. To enrich the congregation's spiritual life;
3. To enable every person to feel a sense of belonging in the church;
4. To provide in-depth caring to shut-ins, the ill, the lonely, the disadvantaged, and the imprisoned;
5. To enhance the development of Christian community, both in the small Care-Groups and in the congregation as a whole;
6. To help with the assimilation of new members;
7. To enable us to celebrate each other's joys and carry each other's burdens;
8. To discover and use the gifts and talents of our people;
9. To improve communication;
10. To keep members active, aware, and involved.

The deacons in the care-ministry program have a direct responsibility to the group coordinators—to help with the training, to give them ongoing support, to hold them accountable so that the program has integrity, and to care for the physical, emotional, and spiritual needs of the coordinators. The deacons are also assigned to Care-Groups so that they are ministered to, like all other group members. The Care-Group coordinators are responsible for convening the groups, helping the groups organize for ministry, and for coordinating the group's effort over a 12-month period. We envision the need to reorganize the groups each year, including the selection of new leaders.

As in any new program, we have had both success and failure. On a scale of 1 to 5 (with 1 as excellent and 5 as poor): I would give three groups a 1; five groups a 3; two groups a 4; and three groups a 5. Difficulties have arisen in groups where too many persons with special needs are in the same group, where too many persons who are less active in the life of the church are in the same group, and where groups have inexperienced leaders who feel overwhelmed by the whole process. We are trying to correct these problems as the program continues; and we may need to consider alternative ways of organizing the groups in the future.

The care-ministry program is the primary work of our Board of Deacons. In addition to this ministry, the deacons assist the pastor with the services of anointing and baptism, provide for the Love Feast and communion twice a year, prepare and serve the Eucharist during worship twice a year, and relate to families at the time of death, including serving a meal for family and friends following the funeral.

Whenever 35 laypersons are willing to be caregivers in a congregation this size, one can assume that significant things are occurring in that congregation. In our case, it is more than an assumption; it is real!

—Allen T. Hansell

Doing What
Can Be Done

York Center Congregation
Lombard, Ill.

The York Center congregation in the Illinois/Wisconsin district is like a good number of other Church of the Brethren congregations in at least one respect. Members of the congregation are extremely busy people. Leaders are often over-extended and can be burned out from too much church work for too long.

"The Office of Deacon" paper (Church of the Brethren Annual Conference 1983) is quite comprehensive in outlining deacon responsibilities. At York Center, it seemed virtually impossible for deacons to assume all of the duties described in that document. So, the deacons made an attempt to keep their duties confined to definite and priority needs in the congregation. As such, some of the responsibilities suggested by the denomination for deacons will not be carried.

The deacons also identified general responsibilities that all deacons accept on request as functions of their office:

1. Assisting with Love Feasts, Sunday morning Eucharist, and baptism when asked by the planning committee;
2. Taking communion to shut-ins and participating in anointing services;
3. Visiting shut-ins intentionally;
4. Doing "special need" visits, as requested, with inactive members, alienated persons, and where there are broken relationships.

Certain functions of the deacons are carried out in subcommittees. Each deacon serves on one of the following committees:

1. Planning for Love Feast, Eucharist, baptism;
2. Overseeing licensed and ordained ministers; this committee represents the congregation in:
   a. identifying persons who should be called;
   b. interviewing on behalf of the congregation; and
   c. seeking ways to deepen both accountability and support with set-apart leadership;
3. Visitation Committee;
4. Caring Committee.

These last two committees adapt to meeting special needs within the congregation. There has been a general congregational visitation and oversight of several existing caring groups. These subcommittees will continue to oversee and/or develop new activities as new needs develop.

At the present time this organization seems to be accomplishing several goals. While "stewarding" the time, energy, and resources of a busy deacon body, it is giving an opportunity for deacons to "do what can be done," and setting aside those things that need not or cannot be done.

If, at some future point, this organization does not fit the York Center congregation, God will hopefully grant to the deacons the insight to acknowledge that condition and the courage to move in a different direction.

—Robert Faus

Section Six:
Appendix

The Office of Deacon
Church of the Brethren Annual Conference Statement

I. INTRODUCTION

The Church of the Brethren has found the Office of Deacon[1] deeply significant throughout its history. One of the set-apart ministries is that of the deacon. The deacon body responds to personal needs and life within the congregation as a part of the church's total ministry. The specific tasks of the deacon body have varied throughout Brethren history.

Brethren are currently experiencing renewed interest in the Office of Deacon. With this interest has come a call for guidance in understanding and structuring the service of deacons in the life of the church.

Currently, the church's practice in calling and commissioning men and women as deacons is quite diverse. Some congregations call members to lifetime service in the Office of Deacon. Other congregations call persons to serve a short term of from three to ten years as members of the deacon body. Still other congregations call some persons to the Office of Deacon for a term, and call others to a life commitment. Likewise, qualifications, tenure, the relation of the deacon body to other groups in the congregational structure, anticipated duties, and the commissioning for office are important enough that the church again seeks to discern and express its common understanding.

II. BIBLICAL THEOLOGICAL BACKGROUND

The root of our word for deacon is found in three major forms in the New Testament: 1) as a verb (*diakoneo* = to serve or minister); 2) as a noun referring to service or ministry done (*diakonia* = service, ministry); and 3) as a noun referring to the person who serves (*diakonos* = minister, servant, or deacon). In only three of these latter cases—Philippians 1:1, 1 Timothy 3:10, and 1 Timothy 3:13—does the text imply that the *diakonos*, the servant or minister, actually has an office. The vast majority of references to *diakonos*, whether singular or plural, male or female (and all are present in the New Testament), refer to any person whose action actually embodies service or ministry.[2]

Our understanding of a deacon—one who serves—is located in our understanding of Jesus himself, who "came not to be served, but to serve" (Mark 10:45). Service and serving is at the heart of Jesus' teaching about his own ministry, as well as about that of his disciples: "Whoever would be great among you, let that one be your servant, and whoever would be first among you, let that one be your slave . . . " (Matt. 20:26b-27). Throughout the gospels Jesus' followers are identified as those who serve others (Matt. 27:55, Mark 15:41, Luke 8:3, Luke 12:37, Luke 17:8, Matt. 25:44). Leaders among Jesus' followers are known in that they served (Luke 22:26). The church understands the basis for the Office of Deacon to be established in the life and ministry of Jesus and Jesus' followers.

This rich inheritance of participation in Christ, as itself being service, gave rise to several specific ministerial offices in the early church: for instance, bishop, presbyter, deacon. Persons called as deacons very early augmented the ministerial leadership in the life of the church (1 Tim. 3, Phil. 1:1). This tradition was retained in the later development of the office. In the post-apostolic church, those called to the Office of Deacon were often the personal assistants of the bishop in conducting public worship, especially at the eucharist and in the administration of church affairs. In the New Testament, deacons were set apart for their ministry. In Acts 6:6 we see that the apostles "prayed and laid their hands upon them," an act signifying God's gift of the Holy Spirit.

---

1. Both men and women hold the Office of Deacon, as both men and women hold the office of pastor.

2. For the remainder of this paper, the word service, serve, or servant will be used each time this Greek root (*diakonos*) occurs. It is equally accurate, however, to read ministry or minister, as both English words are, in these texts, the same word in the New Testament Greek.

As "deacon," "servant," and "minister" are three translations of the same Greek word, there is some question as to whether the early church understood those called to the Office of Deacon to be potential evangelists. Timothy is referred to as God's servant (1 Thess. 3:2). Epaphras is referred to as a faithful servant of Christ (Col. 1:7), Tychicus is named a faithful servant in the Lord (Col. 4:7). Phoebe is described as a servant (*diakonos*) of the church in Cenachrae (Rom. 16:1). Paul uses this same term to refer to his work, as well as that of Apollos. "Who is Paul, and who is Apollos? *Diakonoi* (servants) through whom you believe" (1 Cor. 3:5). Paul again uses the term: "As servant of God we commend ourselves in every way" (2 Cor. 6:4). Steven and Philip, whom we know from Acts 6:1-6 as having been chosen by the early church to serve tables and care for the needs of Hellenist widows, were later known as evangelists.

Guidance in the New Testament as to the qualifications for the Office of Deacon is found in 1 Timothy 3:8-13 (RSV):

> *Deacons, likewise must be serious, not double-tongued, not addicted to much wine, not greedy for gain; they must hold the mystery of the faith with a clear conscience. And let them also be tested first, then if they prove themselves blameless let them serve as deacons. The women likewise must be serious, no slanderers, but temperate, faithful in all things. Let deacons be the husband of one wife, and let them manage their children and their households well; for those who serve well as deacons gain a good standing for themselves and also great confidence in the faith which is in Christ Jesus.*

In our text (and Romans 16:1) we see that both men and women held the Office of Deacon. Women are specifically mentioned in the 1 Timothy text between two occurrences of the plural form of the word for deacon or servant. The qualifications for women who hold the Office of Deacon constitute a general restatement of qualifications already listed in 1 Timothy 3:8 for all deacons. As the marital state of women is not addressed, we assume that it is because women did not enjoy the social freedom to determine their marriage status in the first and second centuries of the early church's life. In the matter of tenure of office, no guidance at all is given in the New Testament. We do know that in the Jewish community and in the apostolic and early post-apostolic era, all set-apart Christian service normally constituted a lifetime commitment, but no lifetime requirements for the office (or any other Christian service) are prescribed in the New Testament.

In summary, the New Testament does not direct us to have deacons, although it is clear that the act of service seen uniquely in Jesus Christ led Jesus' followers likewise to serve, and that the early church did in fact develop the Office of Deacon. The Office of Deacon then, as all offices of ministry, is available to the church insofar as the church's internal needs can be served by calling persons to those specific tasks augmenting the pastoral ministry. Enormous flexibility as to who may serve in the Office of Deacon, what particular service is called for, and length of office for this service is granted in the New Testament. Qualifications for deacons are those we look for in all who serve as ministers of Jesus Christ: a spiritual leader of high moral fiber, trusted and able to give of time and personal compassion and care in the community of faith.

Biblical and Theological Reflections

The New Testament affirms that all members of Christ's body are called to minister according to their gifts (Rom. 12:4-8; 1 Cor. 12:17-31; Eph. 4:11 ff, etc.). Indeed, all gifts are given for the work of service (ministry!) that builds up the body of Christ (Eph. 4:12). But the gifts of, and calls to ministry given to persons by God (Acts 20:24; 2 Cor. 4:1; 2 Cor. 5:18, etc.) were, and presumably are, far more varied than the offices that arose.

Throughout the New Testament, Christian service is understood at its most fundamental level as both participation in and an extension of God's incarnate service in God's world. Service is the whole church's and every Christian's inheritance as coworkers in Jesus Christ's risen presence with us. Thus, more basic than any office of ministry is the fundamental understanding that all who are members of Jesus Christ are called to participate in his service. In addition to this fundamental membership in Christ's body as service, the New Testament recognizes several offices of service to which persons may be called and set apart.

Thus the Church of the Brethren has inherited, cherished and nurtured two traditions from the New Testament church. On the one hand, we speak of the "priesthood of all believers." This is our deep basic affirmation that all members of Jesus Christ's body are called to serve. On the other hand, we have sought, as did the early church, to meet anticipated needs of the body by calling persons to "set-apart" service. This affirmation recognizes with the early church that the congregation needs particular tasks of service to happen in a compassionate, orderly way.

The two sorts of ministry are sometimes considered logically incompatible, but scripturally the priesthood of all believers and set-apart ministries were deeply interdependent. As members of the "priesthood of all believers," all members of the body are called to serve according to the gifts each has been given. In set-apart ministries persons are called—still in accordance with their gifts—to serve particular needs of the local congregation.

Already in the New Testament church, the service of deacons was considered a set-apart ministry, signified in that the apostles "prayed and laid their hands on them" (Acts 6:6b). Brethren also lay hands on persons called to a life commitment to office,[3] in the church's set-apart ministry, whether to the Office of Deacon or to the ordained ministry. Corresponding with the two sorts of ministry visible in the New Testament church and in Brethren heritage, the laying on of hands to signify a life commitment may occur at two significant times in Christian life. The first is at baptism, when God's bestowal of the Holy Spirit is received and celebrated. The second is in commissioning persons to life commitment in the office of set-apart ministry. This second laying on of hands at the time of bestowing office has a double significance. It signifies both God's bestowal of the Holy Spirit and the community's recognition of those gifts of office which lead the community to transfer to those persons significant responsibility for its spiritual nurture.

As we end this section it seems appropriate to comment on our use of the word "deacon." Throughout this paper we will use the word "deacon" to refer both to male and female deacons, except as reference is made to historical documents which use the word "deaconess." We are doing this for two reasons. First, the New Testament uses the same word, *diakonos,* both for men and women who are deacons. We take this as symbolic of the fact that both are to share in the same duties. The use of the same term also implies equal status for both.

The second reason for our use of "deacon" for both genders is that the term of "deaconess" was often used to denote the wife of a deacon who served simply because her husband had been elected a deacon. It was not until the 1956 statement on the Office of Deacon that the word "deaconess" was introduced into our Church of the Brethren vocabulary. This was in recognition that women, as well as men, are called to serve in the Office of Deacon. Yet "deaconess" has been for a long time a technical term for a religious order of women only in other traditions. For this reason we feel that the term does not appropriately apply to women in the Church of the Brethren who are called to the Office of Deacon. The use of the term "deacon" will remove any possible confusion as to whether the female deacon is a fully certified deacon in her own right rather than simply the wife of a deacon.

We are convinced that both men and women can function equally well in the Office of Deacon. Therefore we think the generic word "deacon" should be used with the clear understanding that women, as well as men, are deacons. They should have the same name for their office just as both male and female pastors have the same name for theirs.

III. HISTORICAL BACKGROUND

The Office of Deacon has been an elected position throughout the history of the Church of the Brethren. In accepting the call of the church, the deacon accepted the temporal and spiritual duties of the office.

The 1835 Annual Meeting defined the duties of the Office of the Deacon. As a

---

3. Brethren also lay hands on persons for other reasons than the bestowal of an office of life commitment; for example, when anointing or when calling for or acknowledging the presence of the Holy Spirit, in commissioning the moderator, etc.

"visiting brother," a deacon was to visit, with another deacon, every member prior to the love feast to determine the spiritual state of the congregation and to reconcile differences. A deacon's duties also included supervising love feast preparations and serving the tables during the meals. In relationship to the poor, the deacon was to account for and distribute donated food or money to the congregation's needy, and visit the poor and the sick. Spiritual duties include assisting ministers during meetings by reading scripture and leading prayers. The deacon could lead worship by singing, and within limits, by preaching and making the appointment of subsequent church services if no minister were present to perform this function.

Initially, the deacon was elected to service for life and installed into office by the holy kiss and the extension of the right hand of fellowship. While there was a call in 1848 for the practice of laying on of hands for the installation of deacons, it was not until 1944 that the Annual Conference approved this practice.

In 1866 the question before the Annual Meeting concerned the eligibility of single men to serve as deacons. It was decided that if duly qualified in all other respects, a single man could be elected to hold office.

While it was necessary for a deacon's wife to lead an exemplary life and to stand beside him at the service of installation, it was not until 1956 that the Annual Conference decided that a deacon's wife would be considered a deaconess. That Conference further determined that her term of service coincided with her husband's term; however, in the event of her husband's death, a deaconess could continue to serve in her own right. Conference that year also decided that qualified women could be called to the office of deaconess in their own right and the functions of a deaconess were identical to those of a deacon.

The action of the 1956 Conference also included the following items related to deacons. Local churches were permitted to elect deacons for a definite term of service. The deaconship was to be considered as local church office only and, therefore, a deacon "would not continue as a deacon upon moving into another congregation unless there should be an approving action by the congregation to which he has moved." The action also stated that the deacon board should be related to the church board.

When Annual Conference met in 1960, the delegates were asked whether a person whose baptism was not by trine immersion was qualified to hold the Office of Deacon. The Conference response was to leave this decision to the discretion of local congregations.

Some noteworthy aspects of the 1961 Annual Conference action regarding installation services for term deacons and life deacons include:

- Term deacons shall be "installed by the local church along with other officials who are elected for similar periods of time."
- In regard to life deacon installation services, " . . . it shall be done by a consecration prayer and the laying on of hands . . . "
- Referring to installing term deacons, Conference said, "We recommend . . . the laying on of hands be omitted."

Many of the duties have remained constant, such as the preparing and serving of love feast and communion, ministry to the poor and needy, preparing for baptism, and welcoming new members. However, new roles have been found significant in a growing number of congregations. Under-shepherd plans have been put into practice and some deacon bodies help to maintain accurate membership roles.

IV. QUALIFICATIONS OF OFFICE

Members of the Church of the Brethren qualified to hold the Office of Deacon include men, women, single or married persons and those of all ethnic origins or races, with maturity being more important than chronological age.

The Office of Deacon is a sacred calling to significant ministry. Those called to this office will be persons whose commitment and faithfulness have been proven in relationship to the local fellowship of believers. They will also be persons of a spiritual mind, open and responsive to the Holy Spirit, careful to exercise wisdom and sound judgment while being faithful and loyal to Christ and the church.

Our church looks to deacons to lead exemplary lives and to uphold the doctrines, teachings, and practices of the Church of the Brethren while investing a significant commitment of time, talents, and resources in the congregation's common life.

The loss of any of the above marks of qualification may be reason for a congregation to lose confidence in the ability of a deacon to serve meaningfully, leading the congregation to consider removing that person from the office. Disqualification shall be considered by the congregational business meeting upon recommendation of the executive committee.

As congregations work toward selecting persons to be deacons, they should think in terms of "calling" instead of simply finding someone to fill an office. The function of the deacon is such that the responsibilities will demand a very significant commitment of time and effort. Most of all, congregations need to realize that they are entering into a relationship with their deacons that is similar to their relationship with a pastor and should therefore be treated with the same thoughtfulness and care.

V. ELECTION AND TERM OF OFFICE

Tenure

Deacons may be elected for a term or for life.

Term: We know that historically the deacon was elected to service for life. This practice does and should continue. However, enormous flexibility must be allowed to accommodate the mobility of our times and the unwillingness on the part of some deacon candidates to make a life commitment. Therefore we also feel the need for term deacons. Serving for a term provides for a time of testing. It also provides opportunities for new leadership and fresh energy.

Term deacons may be elected for three-year terms, as is the model for other elected church offices. We recommend that term deacons not be eligible to serve more than two terms in succession and one year must lapse before a deacon can be nominated for another term of service.

Life: Calling deacons to a life of service gives continuous ministry to a congregation. When a congregation calls one from its midst to serve in the capacity of life deacon it means that both parties covenant to be mutually accountable. To work at this accountability life deacons will have a review of their ministry every three years. This review will be facilitated by the executive committee and the pastor. This is similar to the yearly pastoral review.

When a life deacon desires to be declared inactive or when service becomes difficult and the deacon wishes to retire (as ordained ministers retire or claim the emeritus status) the congregation may have a service of affirmation for the service rendered by the deacon.

Method of Nomination and Election

Election of deacons may take place in one of the following ways:

1. An open ballot: In this procedure members vote in congregational business meeting for those they believe qualified, without nominations.

2. A prepared ballot: In this procedure, the nominating and personnel committee prepares for the congregational business meeting a ballot of qualified nominees. Additional names may be presented from the floor.

VI. ORGANIZING AND PERPETUATING THE DEACON BODY

The congregation shall determine the number of active members that make up the deacon body. It is recommended that a congregation consider maintaining a deacon body of one active deacon for every ten active members of the congregation, calling more as necessary to meet the needs of the congregation. Retired deacons may continue to serve in an advisory capacity.

The Office of Deacon is a congregational office and does not automatically transfer when a deacon moves to a new congregation. The call to participate in the deacon body comes as a decision of the congregation based on the individual's qualifications and the needs of the congregation.

The deacon body shall organize itself and choose officers and committees as needed. The chairperson carries out administrative responsibilities and represents the deacon body on the executive committee. A secretary records minutes and keeps the records of the deacon body.

The deacon body is accountable to the executive committee, but may also report directly to the congregational business meeting. The deacon body chairperson serves as a member on the executive committee and the church board by virtue of office, without vote.

The actual ministries of the deacon body and the pastor will at times overlap. The ministry of the church will be best served as the deacon body and the pastor work together. There will be instances when the executive committee can act as facilitator with the pastor and deacons for an effective program of mutual ministry.

The deacon body holds regular meetings. The agenda for these meetings is prepared by the chairperson in consultation with the pastor.

Districts are encouraged to establish a means by which deacon bodies may be called together for any of the following: training, study, fellowship. Any gathering of the deacons on a district level is accountable to the district board. Training events are to be held in the districts, using materials to be developed by the Parish Ministries Commission.

VII. DUTIES OF THE OFFICE OF DEACON

The deacon body's central interest is the spiritual and physical well-being of the church family. Its duties differ significantly from the tasks of commissions, whose responsibilities are expressed in programs aimed to support, nurture, teach, and direct the ministry and mission of all the congregation. In contrast, the deacon body is concerned with the personal needs of congregational members.

In considering the tasks and roles of deacons, it seems wise to express central principles which may guide the executive committee and the deacon body as they consider what concrete practical acts and forms of service will best serve the congregation in any given time and place.

1. Ministry at baptism and assistance with new converts
In cooperation with the custodian, the deacon body assists in the physical preparations and arrangements for the baptismal service.

In working with the pastor, the deacon body is available to assist in arrangements to make the baptismal service a rich and meaningful experience of worship.

The deacon body assists baptismal applicants in preparation for baptism, in entering and exiting from the baptistry, etc. A warm Christian greeting to those who have been baptized is appropriate.

The deacon body cooperates with the pastor in concerns related to the spiritual development and assimilation of the new members.

2. Ministry at the love feast and communion
The deacon body works with the pastor, the moderator, the custodian and others involved in defining clearly the responsibility that each will assume in preparing the meal, the communion bread, the grape juice, the feet washing service, and so forth. Special care is needed to make these services enriching, worshipful experiences.

3. Ministry to the poor and needy in the congregation
The deacon body gives particular attention to the needs of people within the membership and fellowship of the congregation.

4. Ministry to the sick and shut-ins of the congregation
The deacon body is to be especially sensitive to the needs of those who are ill or confined to homes and hospitals. A visitation plan should be arranged in consultation with the pastor so that adequate friendship and support can be given to those particular individuals and families. The deacon body is available to assist the pastor in anointing services or to officiate at anointing services in the pastor's absence.

5. Ministry of reconciliation and restoration
The deacon body, in consultation with the pastor, is available to participate in efforts

to settle differences among members of the congregation. The purpose of such efforts is to (1) bring about the redemption of the individual; (2) preserve the integrity of the church; (3) maintain worthy standards of Christian life and conduct; and (4) nurture loyalty to the church and devotion to Christ. The effort of reconciliation will be carried out in harmony with Matthew 18 and 1 Corinthians 13. Where differences remain unresolved, the District Discipleship and Reconciliation Committee shall be asked to help.

6. Ministry through a shepherding program

It is recommended that each local church consider developing and maintaining a shepherding program so that each member may be part of a small group of caring individuals. The deacon body might well serve as shepherds of those small groups. Such a shepherding program would have the following purposes:

a. To cultivate and keep vital contact with families and individuals of the congregation;

b. To be aware of new families moving into the area;

c. To lead individuals and families to find fellowship in the congregation, while ultimately seeking their commitment to Christ and the church through affiliation with the congregation; and

d. To provide assistance with the ongoing spiritual development and growth of individuals.

Such a shepherding program would require: (1) the division of the congregation into small groups, perhaps geographically, with not more than eight or ten families in each group; (2) enlisting and assigning two members of the deacon body to each group; (3) training by the pastor or other leader in the work to be done; and (4) a simple system of reporting by the shepherds, recording and sharing information as needed. Such a program could serve as a communication system or prayer chain.

7. Ministry to the bereaved

The deacon body, in consultation with the pastor, is available to participate in ministry to the bereaved.

8. Other ministries

We are confident that new forms of ministry will be discovered and that persons in the Office of Deacon will continue to serve the needs of congregations meaningfully.

VIII. A VISION FOR DEACONS

Sections IV through VII have outlined a form for an effective deacon's program in terms of the qualifications and duties of the individual deacons as well as the organizational details for the program as a whole. We feel that any church which conscientiously adopted this program would be enriched and strengthened. Still, we are convinced that the deacons have a calling which is far greater than the minimums expressed above.

We see deacons as vital to the ministry of the church. We see them as an essential part in helping the church, the Body of Christ, to achieve the following qualities: cooperation, communal caring, communication, conflict resolution, and cohesion. Without these properties, our congregations are unlikely to be able to live out the mandates for Christian discipleship according to the New Testament definition of the church.

In the twelfth chapter of 1 Corinthians we see a metaphor for Christian *cooperation*. Deacons need to be a full part of the fabric of church life rather than having their service limited to a few formal functions such as assisting with communion, baptisms, and occasional visits prior to the love feast. As parts of the same body, deacons need to enhance and cooperate with the work of the church's pastors, boards, commissions, and committees. The life of the church can be full only when all of the parts of Christ's body respect and appreciate the various gifts and abilities which others possess. When this is true, all parts of the body can rejoice as each becomes more and more active.

Deacons have traditionally had a key role in working toward our vision of Christian *communal caring*. The sixth chapter of Acts describes the founding of the deacons. The apostles gave to the deacons the responsibility of caring for the physical needs of the widows. Similarly, in the second chapter of Acts we see the whole church sharing material possessions and life space with each other. The life of the church is full only when we too take responsibility for the welfare of our brothers and sisters in Christ. Communal living, as many present-day groups practice it, may not be necessary or even desirable. But the New Testament calls us to have at least the same level of concern for the physical welfare of our fellow church members as commune members have for theirs. Deacons can be instruments of the church's love to needy brothers and sisters when they are supported by the church in this task. Such support needs to include a committed group of willing workers as well as anonymous donors.

As the church struggles for communal caring the need for effective Christian *communication* will become apparent. Sharing each others' lives includes more than the provision for physical needs; it means emotional and spiritual support as well. The deacon's ministry of presence can move in these directions. No pastor alone can do all the ministering that needs to be done. For the sake of Christian communication it behooves the deacon to be present with brothers and sisters on a variety of occasions rather than just in times of crisis. Then, lives can touch in a variety of ways to meet a variety of needs as koinonia is achieved.

Conflict resolution has traditionally been a responsibility of deacons, so it is included in the list of duties above. When deacons are an integral part of the fabric of church life, they can see conflict emerging and can take the risk of facilitating a Christian resolution before a crisis ensues.

Finally, deacons are a vital part of the ministry of *cohesion*. In Matthew 18:22 Jesus teaches about a forgiveness that is the foundation of cohesion. If our congregations are indeed to be churches, we must learn to love our brothers and sisters in spite of their failings. A deacon can serve dual roles as a mediator and as a behavior model. The deacon's life can be a glowing example of creative Christian reconciliation. As brothers and sisters witness this example, the deacon will have little difficulty in establishing possibilities to facilitate reconciliation in others. These reconciliations will increase the bond between the brothers and sisters resulting in Christian *cohesion*.

In summary, we envision the deacons as having a significant ministry in the local church. We see them enhancing cooperation, communal caring, communication, conflict resolution, and cohesion. Moreover we see deacons as actively working at and taking responsibility for the ministry of the church in concert with the pastor or pastors.

IX. COMMISSIONING SERVICE FOR THE OFFICE OF DEACON

This service is to be used when deacons are installed in the Office of Deacon, both for term and life. This may mean a repeat of the service for some deacons who move from term to life. An appropriate sermon shall be preached, setting forth the responsibilities and ministry that belong to this office. In the service of installation, the following passages may be read: Acts 6:1-10; 1 Timothy 3:8-13. Following the sermon, the pastor or other leader entrusted with the service will call the deacons to stand before him/her in the front of the church, facing the chancel. The laying on of hands is an appropriate part of the commissioning service of deacons.

MINISTER: Brothers and sisters in the Lord, the Holy Spirit has directed the church from its very beginning and up to this present hour, to set apart certain persons to look after its temporal interests and to labor for the spiritual unity and growth of the members of Christ's body. These servants are called deacons. Members called to this service are faithful and loyal to God by serving the church. They are spiritually minded, and possess wisdom and discreet judgment in dealing with the affairs of the church. The _____ church, having full confidence in the faithfulness, loyalty, wisdom, and spiritual integrity of Brother _____ and/or Sister _____, according to the practice of the Church of the Brethren, called (him/her) to the Office of Deacon.

The candidates shall kneel while the minister lays hands on them and pray.

Here the candidates shall stand before the minister and before the congregation and answer the questions, make the commitment, and receive their charges.

MINISTER: Forasmuch as the church has called you to assume the Office of Deacon, I now request that you answer the following questions: Do you declare anew your faith in the gospel of our Lord Jesus Christ?

CANDIDATES: I do.

MINISTER: Do you purpose to cultivate more fervently your spiritual life, by Bible reading, meditation, prayer, and Christian witnessing?

CANDIDATES: I do.

MINISTER: Do you purpose to encourage and lead the church in deepening the spiritual life, and in her ministries of compassion?

CANDIDATES: I do.

MINISTER: Do you purpose to be consistent in setting a good example in faith and conduct?

CANDIDATES: I do.

MINISTER: Do you then accept the Office of Deacon in this Body of Christ, and promise to perform faithfully all the duties thereof?

CANDIDATES: I do.

MINISTER: Eternal God, you have given your Spirit to human beings that they may have power for temporal and spiritual service. You have sent your Son not to be served but to serve. Now we set apart and consecrate these your servants to the Office of Deacon, that they may serve in your name. Grant them deep compassion for all human needs; fill them with tender care and steadfast love for every soul for whom Christ died. Inspire them with devotion to your church. Grant them growth in faith that they may lead others by precept and example. Grant to the church grace to work with them for the nurture and the peace of your family. Sustain them through all their labors until their earthly work is done and they are fully with you in your Kingdom. Through Jesus Christ our Lord. Amen.

At the conclusion of the consecration prayer, and after candidates for the Office of Deacon have risen, the officiating minister shall say to them:

MINISTER: In the name of our Lord Jesus Christ, you are now set apart in the sacred Office of Deacon.

Then the minister shall call on the whole church to rise and repeat after him or her the following:

CONGREGATION: We, the members of this Body of Christ, in the spirit of joy, and in renewed loyalty to our Lord, acknowledge and receive you as deacons and promise to pray for and support you in confidence, encouragement, cooperation, and prayers, that together we may increase in the knowledge and the love of God, manifest to us in Jesus Christ our Lord, Amen.[4]

---

4. Adapted from the Book of Worship, 1964.

BACKGROUND OF THE PAPER

The current study of the Office of Deacon was initiated by the General Board in 1980. After consideration by district executives and staff of the General Board, the General Board asked Annual Conference in 1981 to study and bring recommendations for *renewal* of the Office of Deacon, in accord with the current needs and mission of the church. A committee was appointed in 1981 and presented a report to the Annual Conference in 1982. That committee report was then referred by the 1982 Conference to a new committee with instructions to respond to the issues raised in the query and raised by the Annual Conference.

The new committee attempted to address the issues recommended by the 1980 Study Committee, those questions and suggestions resulting from the 1982 Conference hearings and discussions on the Conference floor, and those issues shared in letters received since the 1982 Annual Conference.

In deliberations and in the resulting statement, the committee consciously took into account the biblical setting and teaching, the historical record, current practices, and the needs of the church.

The committee drew extensively on the format and outline of the preceding committee's report. They relied heavily on the meticulous work of the previous committee, especially in sections dealing with historical, biblical, and theological backgrounds for the Office of Deacon.

The paper was adopted by the 1983 Annual Conference.

Copies of this paper are to be available in Spanish, French, and Korean by January 1985.

Estella Horning, Chairperson
Chester I. Harley, Secretary
John L. Huffaker
Mary Jessup
Beth Sollenberger Morphew
Robert S. Over
Samuel Weber-Han
Robert E. Faus, General Board Staff

Sample Materials

SAMPLE--LETTER TO DEACONS

_____
date

TO: Deacon Shepherding Teams

RE: New Assignments

Dear Friends:

Enclosed you will find cards for those families and individuals who have been recently added to your shepherding care. Also enclosed is a copy of the letter which was sent approximately a week ago to the people listed on the new cards. I hope this letter will give you an introduction as their deacon.

I am so grateful for your participation in the shepherding program. It is evident that we are providing much more pastoral care to our church family than ever before. Thank you for helping to make ours a caring congregation.

Sincerely,

_____
pastor

Encl.

P.S. Please call me if you would like additional information about any of your families or individuals.

SAMPLE--LETTER TO CONGREGATIONAL MEMBERS

_____
date

To: Members and Friends regularly associated with _____

name of congregation

From: _____
        pastor

Re: Deacon Shepherding Program

Dear _____:

I am very excited about the expanded ministry of caring at _____ _____ Church that has resulted from our new deacon program. Two years ago the congregation voted to receive the office of deacon and called more than thirty persons to serve as deacons. One of the exciting ministries of this enthusiastic and committed group is a shepherding program in which every person related to our church is assigned to a team of two or three deacons.

These deacon "shepherds" are to keep in touch with the persons in their group, to inform them of special church activities and opportunities, to pray for them, and to be sensitive to any special needs. The deacon shepherds give pastoral care, supplementing the work that I as pastor can do on a limited scale. The deacon shepherd also is a person who can be trusted and called if you have a need or a concern of any kind.

A committee of deacons is charged with the responsibility of 'matching' deacon shepherd teams and individuals or families, but if at any time you would like to request a different team or deacon shepherd, please do not hesitate to call me or _____ who is Deacon Board Chairperson.

Your deacon shepherds as of this date are:

_____ phone_____

Please receive them graciously when they contact you and do not hesitate to call on them for any needs or concerns.

164

SAMPLE--AGENDA FOR INITIAL DEACON VISIT

1. Have a brief time for getting acquainted.

2. Review purpose/function of deacon program and deacon group.

3. Explain the role of the deacon:

   a. To assist persons in making their church membership meaningful.

   b. To make ongoing contacts to inform people as to what is happening in the church.

   c. To be in touch with persons at special/family times, or in crisis.

   d. To be listeners for their concerns/thoughts about the congregation.

   e. As a way of staying in touch, the deacons will make at least one visit to the home a year.

   f. The deacons will have regular meetings for their own support and sharing.

   g. The deacons will assist in welcoming new members into the church fellowship.

4. Share the number of households (and the approximate number of persons) in your deacon group.

5. Hear their ideas/feelings about the deacon program.

6. Invite them to share some life experiences; ask what has been meaningful in their relationship with _____ church.

7. Ask if there is anything further they would like to share about the congregation.

8. Close your visit with each family in a way that feels confortable. Suggestions include: a brief prayer, a friendship circle, a handshake. Do tell them that this has been a meaningful time of sharing, and that you, as their deacons, will keep in touch.

SAMPLE--DEACONS' SHEPHERDING REPORT

Deacon Name(s)_____ Date_____

_____

Check each of the following that applies since the last report.

FAMILY NAME	PHONE CALL	PERSONAL VISIT	CONVER- SATION	OTHER (LIST)	DATE CON- TACT MADE
1._____	_____	_____	_____	_____	_____
2._____	_____	_____	_____	_____	_____
3._____	_____	_____	_____	_____	_____
4._____	_____	_____	_____	_____	_____
5._____	_____	_____	_____	_____	_____
6._____	_____	_____	_____	_____	_____
7._____	_____	_____	_____	_____	_____
8._____	_____	_____	_____	_____	_____
9._____	_____	_____	_____	_____	_____
10._____	_____	_____	_____	_____	_____
11._____	_____	_____	_____	_____	_____
12._____	_____	_____	_____	_____	_____
13._____	_____	_____	_____	_____	_____
14._____	_____	_____	_____	_____	_____

List the name of any families who need extra pastoral care. _____

_____

COMMENTS (Please explain any names listed above.) _____

_____

_____

_____

SAMPLE--DEACON PLANNING SHEET

_____   Date_____
    (Household Name)

Individual   Membership   Current Involvements:
  Names: Status:

_____   _____   _____

_____   _____   _____

_____   _____   _____

_____   _____   _____

_____   _____   _____

Past Contacts: _____

_____

Deacon Plan for 19___

General Objectives for family and/or individuals: _____

_____

Plan for Annual Visit: (Check off
                                                          when done)

   Approximate date desired _____   _____
   Call to make appointment _____   _____
   Actual appointment date _____   _____

Report of Visit:

   General Impressions: _____

   _____

   Specific Comments Noted: _____

   _____

   Next Steps for Deacons: _____

   _____

   Referrals Needed: (to whom, why?) _____

   _____

SAMPLE--COMMISSIONING OF DEACONS
IN SUNDAY MORNING WORSHIP SERVICE

THE PRE-SERVICE MUSIC (as worshippers are seated)
    Ignatius of Loyola used to pause outside
    of a Church before entering it to remember
    into whose presence he was about to come.

THE PRELUDE	O God, Our Help in Ages Past	Craft

THE CALL TO WORSHIP
THE INVOCATION

*HYMN	Come, Thou Fount of Every Blessing	438

THE WELCOME AND SHARING OF JOYS AND CONCERNS
THE CHILDREN'S STORY
A PRAYER LITANY (on back of bulletin)

AN ANTHEM	Praise Ye the Lord	Franck

THE SCRIPTURE LESSON		I Timothy 3:8-13
*HYMN	Thou My Everlasting Portion	482

THE SERMON	A CALL TO THE SERIOUS LIFE	
AN ANTHEM	Create In Me a Clean Heart, O God	Mueller

THE COMMISSIONING OF DEACONS
  Introductory Statements
  Vows and Commitment
  Prayer of Consecration
 *Congregational Response (in unison)
    We, the members of this body of Christ, in the
    spirit of joy, and in renewed loyalty to our Lord,
    acknowledge and receive you as deacons and promise
    to pray for and support you in confidence, encour-
    agement, cooperation, and prayers, that together
    we may increase in the knowledge and the love of
    God, manifest to us in Jesus Christ our Lord. Amen.

THE OFFERING
  The Invitation to Give

Offertory Music	Bless, O Lord, This Church of Thine	
*HYMN OF DEDICATION	Because I Have Been Given Much	340

*THE BENDICTION

*CHORAL RESPONSE	May Grace, Mercy and Peace

(The commissing service itself is found in the Office of
Deacon, Church of the Brethren Annual Conference
Statement, pp. 9-10.)

SAMPLE--SUGGESTIONS FOR DEACON SHEPHERDS

1. Who Are the Flock?
   a. People of varying relationships to the church
   b. People for whom our church has responsibility
   c. People for whom Jesus cares

2. What Does Caring Mean?
   a. We consider them a part of our church family
   b. We expect them to be participating members
   c. We want the church to be helpful to them
   d. We want them to have an enabling faith

3. How to Get Started:
   a. Pray for your flock
   b. Watch and listen for news about your group members
   c. Get acquainted with everyone in your flock
   d. Make your own notes of what caring means for each family/individual
   e. Choose the kind of contact that seems most effective
   f. Look for your flock at church
   g. Keep your flock informed of church activities
   h. Be ready and willing to respond to special needs of your flock
   i. Keep pastor informed of any special needs

4. Some "Do"s and "Don't"s for Making Contacts:
   DO look for ways to be complimentary of the other
   DO seek and affirm common ground with the other
   DO talk positively about the church
   DO recall any contributions the other has made to the church
   DO invite to church school, worship, and other functions
   DO be above board with the purpose of your contact
   DO remember you represent the church, but foremost be a friend
   DO feel free to pray with the other
   DO ask if they would like the pastor to call (if this seems appropriate)
   DO report to the pastor or appropriate official any helpful information
   DO enjoy your contact

   DON'T be too aggressive (listen with love)
   DON'T use knowledge of others for gossip
   DON'T put the other on the defensive
   DON'T apologize for any ministry of the church
   DON'T argue with criticism/complaints
   DON'T feel that you have to solve all the problems

5. Some Thoughts For Making a Contact:

"I'm sure you've read or heard that we have a new deacon program at church, and _____ and I have been chosen to be your deacon shepherds. We're interested in helping to make the church a place where you can express your faith and find spiritual resources for everyday. We think church members ought to care more about one another. I'm sure you'd agree with that....We haven't had a way to keep in touch regularly with our church members and we hope the deacon shepherding program will help make that better.

_____ or I will be checking with you periodically, but in the meantime if there's any way we or the church can be helpful please let us know. You're important to us and we need you as much as you need the church."

Section Seven:
Annotated Bibliography

Bibliography

Anointing: The Congregation's Use of Anointing for Healing and Reconciliation, by Dean M. Miller. Elgin: Brethren Press, 1987.
"Looks at the crucial role of the faith community in healing; presents ways the congregation can become more intentional about its role in healing and wholeness."

Anointing Packet. Elgin: Brethren Press, 1987.
"Resources lifting up the central role that spirituality and faith have in health and healing in real-life circumstances; includes biblical study, worship resources, sermons, pamplet and booklet on anointing."

Anointing Videotape: "Is Any Among You Suffering?" Elgin: Brethren Press, 1987.
"Presents the anointing service as a spiritual treasure which the church holds; examines both private and public approaches to the service, and shares the reflections of persons for whom anointing has had special meaning."

The Apathetic and Bored Church Member, by John S. Savage. Reynoldsburg, Ohio: LEAD Consultants, 1976.
"Presents the premise that most inactive members have become inactive because the congregation has not heard their cries for help." (Also helpful for those who visit church members is Savage's training lab, "Skills for Calling and Caring Ministries.")

The Care and Feeding of Volunteers, by Douglas W. Johnson. Nashville: Abingdon, 1978.
"This work, which is part of the Creative Leadership Series, is an excellent reminder of the manner in which pastors might support and nurture the work of deacons who are, among other things, volunteers."

The Caring Church: A Guide for Lay Pastoral Care, by Howard W. Stone. New York: Harper and Row, 1983.
"An excellent training guide for lay pastoral care; includes a discussion of the why of lay pastoral care, the organization of a program, and eight excellent training sessions."

Celebration of Discipline: The Path to Spiritual Growth, by Richard J. Foster. New York: Harper and Row, 1978.
"Presents the importance of each Christian's developing a deeper inner life; uses classical spiritual disciplines as a way of becoming open to the presence of God."

Christian Caregiving—A Way of Life, by Kenneth C. Haugk. Minneapolis: Augsburg Publishing House, 1984. (A leaders' guide was developed in 1986.)
"A presentation of the essential dimensions of caregiving by the founder of the Stephen Series, a highly acclaimed training program for lay ministers." (For information on the training program, write to Stephen Ministries, 1325 Boland, St. Louis, MO 63117.)

Compassion: A Reflection on the Christian Life, by Donald P. McNeill, Douglas A. Morrison, and Henri Nouwen. Garden City, NY: Doubleday, 1983.
"This excellent work covers the biblical understanding of compassion, which lies at the heart of all Christian caregiving."

Comprehensive Pastoral Care, by Samuel Southard. Valley Forge, PA: Judson Press, 1975.
"Vividly portrays the role deacons can take in pastoral care; helpful models and memorable illustrations; highly recommended."

The Dynamics of Discipleship Training, by Gary W. Kuhne. Grand Rapids: Zondervan Publishing House, 1978.
"An integration of psychology and scripture designed to enable young Christians to grow to maturity."

Forgive and Forget, by Lewis B. Smedes. New York: Harper & Row, 1984.
"A challenging book on the healing power of forgiveness."

Healing Life's Hurts, by Matthew Linn and Dennis Linn. Mahwah, NJ: Paulist Press, 1978.
"How to find healing for injuries received through life; guidance on healing of memories through the stages of forgiveness."

How to Mobilize Church Volunteers, by Marlene Wilson. Minneapolis: Augsburg Publishing House, 1983.
"Pertinently-described ways to call forth and equip lay persons; also includes excellent lists of varied ministries in which lay persons can be meaningfully involved."

Improving Your Serve, by Charles Swindoll. Waco, Texas: Word Books, 1981.
"The art of unselfish living; characteristics and lifestyle of a servant."

Lay Caregiving, by Diane Detwiler-Zapp and William Coveness Dixon. Philadelphia: Fortress Press, 1982.
"Building on a theology of ministry that includes all Christians, this book describes the practical steps in developing training for lay caregivers in the church."

Learning to Share the Ministry, by James R. Adams and Celia A. Hahn. Washington, D.C.: Alban Institute Publications.
"How clergy and laity in one church learned to share the ministry, with the pastor's sabbatical as an important stimulus; has a helpful study guide."

Let My People Go, by Alvin J. Lindgren and Norman Shawchuck. Nashville: Abingdon Press, 1980.
"Provides encouragement and guidance on how clergy can empower the laity for ministry."

My Struggle to Be a Caring Person, by Celia Allison Hahn, James R. Adams, and Amy Anne Gavin. Washington, DC: Alban Institute Publications, 1981.
"An organization and training manual from one congregation's program to provide lay caregiving. Though not called "deacons" the lay persons in this model function in a similar way to deacon caregivers."

The Passionate People, by Keith Miller and Bruce Larson. Waco, Texas: Word Books, 1979.
"A 'how to' and 'a how to be' book, revealing a person's hidden resources to become a change agent in the lives of others."

Pastoral Psychology 30 (Summer 1982). "Pastoral Care and the People of God," by Russell Burck, pp. 139-152.
"Emphasizes the need to shift from a professional to a congregational model of care and affirm the giftedness and ministries of all the people of God."

Peer Counseling; An In-Depth Look at Training Peer Helpers, by H. Dean Gray and Judy A. Tindal. Muncie, IN: Accelerated Development, Inc., 1978.
"A detailed description of how to train people in the practical skills of communication, conflict resolution, and problem solving."

Recovery of Ministry, A Guide for the Laity, by Orien Johnson. Valley Forge, PA: Judson Press, 1972.
"Addresses the vital importance of having lay persons assume ownership of ministry."

Repairing the Breach, by Ronald S. Kraybill. Scottdale: Herald Press, 1982.
"A guide to understanding and working at conflict within the church and the community."

Resolving Our Differences: The Church's Ministry of Reconciliation by Lynn and Juanita Buzzard. Elgin: David C. Cook Publishing Co., 1982.
"Presents the case for the church's need to be involved in reconciliation; includes eight training sessions."

The Second Greatest Commandment, by William M. Fletcher. Colorado Springs, CO: Navpress, 1983.
"A call to a personal and corporate life of caring; includes a careful study of the Biblical basis for caring."

Spiritual Gifts Tendency Questionnaire. Available from Broadway Baptist Church, 3931 Washington, Kansas City, MO 64111.
"A very useful exercise for deacons and others."

Stretcher Bearers, by Michael Slater. Oxnard, CA: Regal Books, 1985.
"Practicing and receiving the gift of encouragement and support."

Supportive Care in the Congregation, by Dean A. Preheim-Bartel and Aldred H. Neufeldt. Akron, PA: Mennonite Central Committee, 1986.
"A congregational care plan for providing a supportive care network for persons who are disabled or dependent."

Telecare Ministry, by Harald Grindal. Minneapolis: Augsburg, 1984.
"A very helpful resource on using the telephone in a care ministry."

Tell It to the Church, by Lynn Buzzard and Lawrence Eck. Carol Stream, IL: Tyndale House Publishing, 1985.
"Looks at the church's responsibilty regarding peacemaking between persons."

When A Congregation Cares: A New Approach to Crisis Ministry, by Abraham and Dorothy Schmitt. Scottdale: Herald Press, 1986.
"A practical description of how a congregation can organize to minister to the crisis needs which often overwhelm a church."

When A Congregation Cares: Videotape. Herald Press.
"Presents the concept of a caring team as a way for churches to use the gifts of lay members in ministry to others; includes questions for group discussion."

The Wounded Healer, by Henri Nouwen. Garden City, NY: Doubleday, 1979.
"Lifts up the vital role of the healer who has been equipped through the experience of being wounded and discovering the redemptive grace of God and community."